P R A Y E R

SHIELD

I BELIEVE THAT OF ALL THE BOOKS I HAVE WRITTEN, THIS will be the most important one for pastors and other Christian leaders.

Why? Because it really works! As I have shared this information about personal intercession verbally over the years, many pastors have told me that taking my suggestions has literally transformed their ministry.

This is an instruction manual for both leaders and lay people. It will help form new relationships anointed by God for setting His people free to be all He wants them to be.

C. Peter Wagner

It is imperative that we learn how to pray effectively for our leaders—in churches, in organizations, and in prayer movements. *Prayer Shield* is both timely and definitive. There's nothing else quite like it, designed to equip all of us to bring the covering of the Lord upon the servants of the Lord, by prayer. This is a book that must be read, now more than ever.

David Bryant, President, Concerts of Prayer International

Prayer Shield is the most inspirational book I have ever read on the subject of intercession.

Suzette Hattingh, Prayer Leader for Reinhard Bonnke

In *Prayer Shield*, Peter Wagner opens a whole new area of prayer concern. As I read this book, I wondered how we had missed this crucial area. It's so obvious that those who bear the brunt of ministry need spiritual support. But oh, how to find it!

Dr. Walter Wink, Professor, Auburn Theological Seminary

I want to give this book to every member of my church.

Rick Warren, Pastor,
Saddleback Valley Community Church, Mission Viejo, CA

C. PETER WAGNER

PRAYER SHIELD

HOW TO INTERCEDE FOR PASTORS, CHRISTIAN LEADERS AND OTHERS ON THE SPIRITUAL FRONTLINES

Regal

A Division of Gospel Light
Ventura, California, U.S.A.

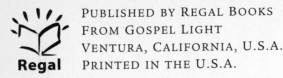

PUBLISHED BY REGAL BOOKS
FROM GOSPEL LIGHT
VENTURA, CALIFORNIA, U.S.A.
PRINTED IN THE U.S.A.

Regal

Regal Books is a ministry of Gospel Light, a Christian publisher dedicated to serving the local church. We believe God's vision for Gospel Light is to provide church leaders with biblical, user-friendly materials that will help them evangelize, disciple and minister to children, youth and families.

It is our prayer that this Regal book will help you discover biblical truth for your own life and help you meet the needs of others. May God richly bless you.

For a free catalog of resources from Regal Books/Gospel Light, please call your Christian supplier or contact us at 1-800-4-GOSPEL or www.regalbooks.com.

Scripture quotations in this book are taken from the *New King James Version*, Holy Bible. Copyright © 1979, 1980, 1982 by Thomas Nelson, Inc., Publishers. Used by permission.

Library of Congress Cataloging-in-Publication Data

Wagner, C. Peter.
    Prayer shield : how to intercede for pastors, Christian leaders and others on the spiritual frontlines / C. Peter Wagner.
        p. cm.
    Includes index.
    ISBN 0-8307-1514-2 (trade paper)
    1. Intercessory prayer. 2. Clergy—Religious life. I. Title.
BV215.W33 1992
248.3'2—dc20   92-20858
                                                                      CIP

23 24 25 26 27 28 29 30 31 32 / 13 12 11 10 09 08 07 06 05 04

Rights for publishing this book in other languages are contracted by Gospel Light Worldwide, the international nonprofit ministry of Gospel Light. Gospel Light Worldwide also provides publishing and technical assistance to international publishers dedicated to producing Sunday School and Vacation Bible School curricula and books in the languages of the world. For additional information, visit www.gospellightworldwide.org; write to Gospel Light Worldwide, P.O. Box 3875, Ventura, CA 93006; or send an e-mail to info@gospellightworldwide.org.

Lovingly dedicated to the

Irons family

Alex and Ruth

Katherine, Joshua and Herbert

Contents

PRAYER
SHIELD

Introduction

FEW CHRISTIANS NOTICED WHEN AROUND 1970 A GREAT NEW prayer movement began sweeping through Christian churches worldwide. Nowadays few remain unaware. Never before, in living memory, has prayer been such a high agenda item for pastors, Christian leaders and ordinary believers in the pews.

I was among those who were unaware in 1970. As I will explain later, that was just the time when I was entering the most prayerless period of my ministry. I then began relearning and experiencing the power of prayer in the early 1980s when I started the adult Sunday School class I teach in Lake Avenue Congregational Church in Pasadena, California. The process was slow at first, but I switched to the fast track in 1987.

Beginning in 1980, I was drawn to prayer as part of an attempt of trying to understand the spiritual dimensions of church growth. I am known to many as a professor of church growth at Fuller Seminary and I give much of my life to analyzing why it is that some churches grow while others decline and die. For years, I dealt primarily with what are institutional factors and contextual factors. More recently, however, I am also attempting to understand the spiritual factors that influence the growth of churches.

In 1987, I began giving major attention to prayer. I did what professors frequently do, and began collecting a personal library on the subject. I now own and have read scores of volumes, and feel as though I have a fairly good grasp of the field. One of the reasons why I go about it this way is to discover which specific areas in the entire field of prayer have been relatively neglected in the past. This helps me set my personal research priorities.

Three obvious vacancies in the literature emerged: (1) strategic-level intercession or spiritual warfare dealing with principalities and powers, (2) intercession for Christian leaders, and (3) the relationship between prayer and the growth of the local church. I am in the process of writing a new book on each of these subjects, plus another in the series on the crucial subject of spiritual mapping. The book on strategic-level intercession, *Warfare Prayer* (Regal Books) is now available. This book deals with intercession for leaders, and the third and fourth are yet to come.

I had been learning about personal intercession for leaders mainly through experience for a few years before beginning my research. As a result of personally receiving intercession, my ministry had moved to a plane higher than it had ever been before. Because of this I was quite surprised to discover that many of those who had been teaching on prayer were not talking much about praying for pastors or other leaders.

In former generations, a small amount of teaching on intercession for leaders was available. More than 100 years ago, for example, Charles G. Finney dedicated two pages of his classic, *Lectures on Revivals of Religion*, to admonish his readers to "Pray for your minister." Among other things, he said, "I have known a church to bear their minister on their arms in prayer from day to day and watch, with anxiety unutterable, to see that he has the Holy Ghost with him in his labors!" And later, "How different is the case, where the church feels that their *minister* is praying, and so there is no need of their praying!"[1]

Quite predictably, E. M. Bounds, the one person who has probably written more on prayer than anyone else, has something to say about praying for pastors. A chapter in his *Power Through Prayer* (1912) is, "Preachers Need the Prayers of the People"; and one in *The Weapon of Prayer* (1931) is, "The Preacher's Cry: 'Pray for Us!'" Bounds considers prayer for pastors so important that he says, "Air is not more necessary to the lungs than prayer to the preacher." He stresses, as I do in this book, *"the preacher must pray; the preacher must be prayed for"* (emphasis his).[2]

Of the contemporary authors who write on prayer, two who write on intercession for leaders both happen to be personal prayer partners for my wife, Doris, and me. The first is Dick Eastman, who admonishes us to "cover those already laboring in the harvest" and gives us what he calls ten "Colossian claims" for Christian workers.[3]

The other is Cindy Jacobs who writes an entire chapter on "Personal Prayer Partners." Among other things, she tells of problems she and her husband, Mike, were experiencing with their ministry, Generals of Intercession. The problems turned around 180 degrees when they enlisted the help of prayer partners.[4]

An example of a pastor who writes on intercession for leaders is Michael Tucker in his book, *The Church That Dared to Change* (Tyndale).

Although not a book per se, John Maxwell, pastor of Skyline

Wesleyan Church of San Diego, California, has an excellent video and audiocassette tape resource called *The Pastor's Prayer Partners.*[5] This is an outstanding resource, which I highly recommend. I know of no one more qualified to present this resource than my friend John, who has recruited 100 highly committed men to pray for him on an intense and ongoing basis.

A further resource, which includes one video and six audiocassettes, is my own *How to Have a Prayer Ministry.*[6] It contains some material you will find in this book, and some you will not.

To my knowledge, this is the first book entirely focused on the area of pastors and their personal prayer partners. In this book I use "pastors" in the broader sense to include Christian leaders in general, as I am. Although people such as Billy Graham, James Dobson, Loren Cunningham and Peter Wagner need intercessory prayer perhaps even more than do some local church pastors, the Christian leaders to whom most Christian people directly relate day in and day out are their pastors. That is why I am giving pastors such a high profile.

This book is not just for the pray-ers. It is also for those who receive the prayers. One of my central purposes is to help pastors and leaders understand their intercessors, and the intercessors understand the Christian leaders they are praying for. As this begins to happen, I believe awesome quantities of new divine power will be released through our churches, parachurch organizations and other ministries for the advancement of the Kingdom of God here on earth.

Notes

1. Charles G. Finney, *Lectures on Revivals of Religion* (New York, NY: Fleming H. Revell Company, 1868), p. 224.

2. E. M. Bounds, *The Complete Works of E. M. Bounds on Prayer* (Grand Rapids, MI: Baker Book House, 1990), p. 486.
3. Dick Eastman, *Love on Its Knees* (Old Tappan, NJ: Chosen Books, 1989), p. 118.
4. Cindy Jacobs, *Possessing the Gates of the Enemy* (Tarrytown, NY: Chosen Books, 1991), pp. 156-171.
5. John Maxwell, *The Pastor's Prayer Partners* (available from Injoy Ministries, 1530 Jamacha Rd., Suite D, El Cajon, CA 92019, 1-800-333-6506).
6. C. Peter Wagner, *How to Have a Prayer Ministry* (available from the Charles E. Fuller Institute, Box 91990, Pasadena, CA 91109-1990, 1-800-999-9587).

The Power of Personal Prayer Partners

E

THE REASON I AM WRITING THIS BOOK IS THAT I AM PER-
sonally convinced the following statement is true:
The most underutilized source of spiritual power in
our churches today is intercession for Christian leaders.

I purposely did not say "one of the most underutilized sources of power" because I do not think anything
else this important is actually so neglected. We do not
do it, and we usually do not even talk about it.

I do not mean to imply that intercession for our leaders is the only source of spiritual power in churches.
No. The proclamation of the Word, prayer, worship,
praise, healing, confession, fasting, the sacraments, spiritual gifts and many other significant sources of spiritual power are currently being used in churches. True,
many of them are not being used as well or as fre-

quently as we might like, but they are there and we recognize them. Not so with intercession for our leaders.

I will show you what a difference it can make.

SPIRITUAL BRINKMANSHIP AT SKYLINE WESLEYAN

One of my closest friends is Pastor John Maxwell of Skyline Wesleyan Church in San Diego. I will mention him frequently in this book because I have learned so much from him about pastors' personal prayer partners. In his church, unlike most others, intercession for leaders is utilized to the maximum. It is woven into the very warp and woof of the church's philosophy of ministry.

Maxwell firmly believes that because of intercessory prayer the church narrowly averted a major mistake. Not that it might have led to a total disaster, but it clearly would have set the church on a track that would not have allowed it to be all God wanted it to be.

For several years under John Maxwell's leadership, God blessed the church with substantial growth. By the time it had grown to around 3,000 people, the old facilities located in a deteriorating section of the city had been stretched beyond capacity. Three services on Sunday morning could not hold all who wanted to attend; so as would be expected the growth plateaued. It was obvious to all that if the church was to reach all the people God had called them to reach they would have to move to new facilities.

Finding a new site large enough for their bold, God-given vision for the future was no easy task in greater San Diego. They knew they needed up to 100 acres in a desirable area. Real estate agents were telling them San Diego had experienced so much recent growth that this kind of property simply was no longer available. They should have looked for it 10 or 15 years previously.

John Maxwell has 100 men from his church who are highly

committed to pray for him. In due time I will explain how this came about, but suffice it to say at the moment that these men were praying with John and his leaders as they began the search for the new property. Month after month went by, frustration after frustration piled up, and morale began to slip. The church continued on the plateau, although its true growth potential remained as high as ever. It began to look as if the real estate agents were right.

Then a breakthrough came. A 50-acre piece of prime real estate located right on the freeway became available. John's team went to work, struggled through some tough negotiations and finally made an offer of $2 million, which the owner accepted. John and his church board felt they had looked at all the angles and were convinced it was the right move. They set a Sunday night for a congregational meeting to receive and approve the board's recommendation that they purchase the land for their future site.

But even with all the prayer that had gone up over the months, John characteristically wanted to make sure they had prayed enough. After all, it would be one of the most momentous decisions the church had ever made or would ever make, and he and the other leaders wanted to be absolutely certain it was God's will. So Maxwell said to his prayer partners, "Let's make sure, guys, that we have reached the right decision. Just in case, let's all go out to the property and pray once again."

"This Is Not Your Site!"

On the Saturday before the crucial congregational meeting, John Maxwell and his 100 prayer partners went out to what they believed would be the future site of Skyline Wesleyan. The more they prayed, the more they began getting a strange feeling, first individually, then in groups. After unimaginable agonizing, they began to admit to each other that collectively they were hearing God say, "This is not your site!"

At the congregational meeting the next evening, John rehearsed the process they had gone through to decide to purchase the property. It had seemed right from the business point of view, from the financial point of view, from the church management point of view, and from advice they had received from many sources. But one thing could outweigh all those positive indications—the word from the Lord received through earnest and effective prayer.

Even though Maxwell knew that many would be disappointed, he had built up enough faith in the hand of God working in his life and the life of the church through his prayer partners that he became bold. He recommended that Skyline Wesleyan Church withdraw the offer for the property. He also assured the congregation that if God was really telling them not to buy this property, it was because He had something much better in store for them. How much better no one could have imagined at the time!

The search process began once again. They located a beautiful 80-acre property and asked the owners twice if they would sell, but they were turned down both times. The prayer partners and others continued to pray. Soon a financial crunch came and the owners seemed more disposed to sell. Skyline made a very low bid of $1.8 million for the 80 acres, and the owners by then were in such a tight situation they reluctantly said they would sell. But the owners insisted on some fine print: If Skyline could not get the land zoned for a church, they would agree not to sell the land but would return the land and also pay the owners interest on the amount Skyline had spent.

The church, cognizant of the risk, closed the deal only to find out through an independent appraiser that the true value of the land was $4.5 million. Skyline Church had taken an even greater risk than they thought!

Turning 80 Acres into 130

The church was also forced to buy three times the number of shares of water rights than necessary, and they paid $120,000 for them. But drought set in on Southern California, the value of the water rights soared, and the owners begged them to sell two-thirds of the rights back. By that time the two-thirds were worth $250,000 and as part of the deal, the church persuaded the former owners to rescind the clause that they would have to give back the property if it were not zoned for their use. So God gave them the property for the price they had offered with no fine print, along with an extra $130,000!

But that is not all. They had the "80 acres" surveyed and found that the land was really 110 acres! Then the Water District needed 10 acres on the low part of the land and offered to trade 30 acres at the top, right where John Maxwell had envisioned the parking lot, for the 10. They now had 130 acres. Finally they were offered $4 million for a stretch of industrially-zoned land, which they did not need for the church anyway.

Skyline Wesleyan now has a lovely church site, probably worth more than $10 million, for which they ended up not paying a thing!

This was all because of prayer. Through prayer, the pastor's prayer partners had heard God say, No. Their spiritual maturity caused them to be bold enough to follow what they knew would be an unpopular course of action. Once they followed, they began hearing a series of yesses from God that carried them, their pastor, the church board and the congregation over the threshold and into the greatest era of Skyline Wesleyan's history.

My point is that Skyline Wesleyan Church does not have an exclusive franchise on this kind of prayer power. God wants to release similar power in your church as well, and this book will help you tune in to the ways and means of seeing it released. The best days for you, your pastor and your church might also be just ahead!

HOW GOD'S POWER IS RELEASED

A fascinating story is told in Exodus 17. Many will recall the account of the battle of Rephidim in which Joshua defeated Amalek. Joshua's name has been entered permanently into military history as the general who won the battle of Rephidim.

But the Bible tells us the rest of the story.

A strategy conference before the battle had determined that while Joshua would lead the troops out to the battlefield, Moses would go up on a nearby hill and intercede for Joshua. On the hill overlooking the battle, Moses soon observed that while his hands were up, Joshua was winning, but while his hands were down, Joshua was losing. Moses caught on real fast and decided that the best place for his hands was up. So Aaron and Hur came to help, propped Moses up with stones, and did everything they could to keep Moses' hands in the air. As a result, Joshua won the battle (see Exod. 17:8-13).

This is a simple story and has a great principle for us to grasp. Joshua is fighting while Moses is praying. Joshua gets credit for winning the battle, but we know who really won it. Ultimately, of course, it was God's power that won the battle, but the human agent most directly used as a channel of that divine power was the intercessor, Moses, not the general, Joshua.

As my friend Walter Wink would say, "history belonged to the intercessor."[1]

As I apply this to real life, I see Joshua doing the "ministry." It so happened that his God-given assignment at the moment was to fight a battle. I wonder just how much Joshua was praying throughout that day in the Valley of Rephidim. Probably not much, if at all. Yet the battle was ultimately won by prayer, the prayers of the intercessor, not the prayers of the minister. Not that Joshua was unimportant. The battle could not have been won without him either.

Many Christian leaders today are like Joshua. They are activists in the ministry. They are winners. People see them as successful servants of God. Day after day they see God's power operating through them for the blessing of others. And where does this power come from? It is released through intercession.

REVIVAL IN HEREFORD, TEXAS

One of the first real life experiences of the power of personal intercession I heard came from my friend Larry Lea. He had just finished seminary and was serving as youth minister in Beverly Hills Baptist Church in Dallas. The church was growing well, and so was Larry's youth group. He had 1,000 teenagers in his group and it was one of the largest in the area. It was then that he received his first invitation to do a citywide evangelistic crusade. The city was Hereford, Texas; population 15,853. Lea had felt that one of his stronger gifts was that of an evangelist and he had great faith that God would give him a significant harvest of souls in Hereford.

The format was the type of citywide crusade in which the evangelist would preach each night in a different one of the cooperating churches. The first night he preached his heart out but no one responded to the invitation. When the same thing happened the second night, Larry Lea began to worry. "What's going on? I know my sermons are decent. They are theologically sound. The gospel is clear. What will I say when I get back to Dallas and report to my youth group?"

The third night the meeting was to be held in the Methodist church. Larry had arrived a bit early when two women approached him. They saw he was nervous so they said, "Don't worry, Brother Lea. We've prayed for you today for eight hours." They asked if they could lay on hands and pray for him there. When they finished, one of the women said to him, "Does the phrase 'It is finished' mean anything to you?" It was Larry's text for the evening! He preached and 100 responded to the invitation!

The next night Larry looked for the two women. They prayed for him again, and the other woman asked him if he remembered the woman with the issue of blood. Again, it was the text he had chosen for that evening!

Before the week was over, 500 had responded to the preaching and had made decisions for Christ. Larry was elated. On the flight back to Dallas he began rehearsing how he would share the good news of his successful crusade with his youth group. Then in a quiet moment Lea clearly heard the voice of God coming to him and saying, "Son, you had nothing to do with that revival. The reason those people got saved was that somebody *prayed the price!*"

It was there and then that Larry Lea learned the value of personal intercession for leaders. He was the Joshua on the battlefield, in this case the evangelist who went down in history as seeing 500 come to Christ in Hereford, Texas. But the power of God came primarily through the two women who, like Moses, faithfully did the work of intercession.[2]

WHAT IS INTERCESSION?

We often use the word "intercession" as a synonym for "prayer." In ordinary conversation it is acceptable to use the words interchangeably, but not when we are dealing with them as technical terms. Prayer, generally speaking, means talking to God. Intercession is coming to God on behalf of another. All intercession is prayer, but not all prayer is intercession.

"Intercession" is derived from the Latin *inter*, meaning "between" and *cedere*, meaning "to go." Intercession, then, is going between or standing in the gap. Through Ezekiel the prophet, the Lord says, "I sought for a man among them who would make a wall, and stand in the gap before Me on behalf of the land, that I should not destroy it; but I found no one" (Ezek. 22:30). This is a clear reference to intercession.

To put it theologically: "Intercession is the act of pleading by one who in God's sight has a right to do so in order to obtain mercy for one in need."[3] This makes the important point that

---

Intercession is coming to God on behalf of another. All intercession is prayer, but not all prayer is intercession.

---

the standing of the person before God qualifies or disqualifies the potential intercessor.

The book of Esther provides us with a powerful biblical analogy of the function of an intercessor.

The story itself is well known. The mighty king of Persia, more than 400 years before Christ, was called Ahasuerus in Hebrew and Xerxes in Greek. He ruled the whole Middle East from India to Ethiopia. Ahasuerus falls in love with the beautiful Jewess, Esther, and makes her queen without knowing she is a Jew. Meanwhile, Haman, captain of the princes, becomes infuriated when Esther's uncle Mordecai refuses to bow to him. Discovering that Mordecai is a Jew, Haman vengefully plots a holocaust "to destroy, to kill, and to annihilate all the Jews" in all the provinces of Persia (Esther 3:13). Mordecai gets wind of the plot and asks Esther to intervene with Ahasuerus on behalf of her people.

The custom of those days prohibited anyone, even a queen, to initiate an audience with the king. One should speak to a king only when spoken to. Violation of this protocol incurred the death penalty. But Esther risked her life and told the king of Haman's wicked intentions. The king responded favorably, executed Haman, and then worked around the laws of the Medes and Persians so that the Jewish people were saved.

How is this an analogy for intercession?

First, Ahasuerus, politically speaking, was omnipotent within his kingdom. In that respect he represents God. Haman rep-

---

Intercessors are not manipulators of God, and some things God has set in concrete.

---

resents Satan who comes to steal, to kill and to destroy. Esther is the intercessor, the one who "stands in the gap." Mordecai takes the role of the Holy Spirit in communicating the will of God in the matter to Esther.

In the course of this book I will name and describe many real-life contemporary intercessors. They bear an astounding resemblance to Esther. Esther was humble, not arrogant. She was submissive to authority. She was tuned in to the voice of God and willing to obey what she heard even at the risk of her life. She was dependent on what we would now refer to as the Body of Christ, asking her fellow Jews to support her in prayer and fasting. She herself also fasted for three days. When she felt in tune spiritually, she was ready to say, "I will go to the king, which is against the law; and if I perish, I perish!" (Esther 4:16).

When Esther approached the throne of the king, she was welcomed because of a previously developed love relationship. A special intimacy with God is high on the profile of intercessors. As a result, the king used his power to save the people of God. As today's intercessors testify, the highest reward of the ministry of intercession is to be received in love by the Father and to see His power released for good through their intervention.

HOW POWERFUL ARE THESE PETITIONS?

Some may ask: Do you really mean that the petition of a mere human being can determine the actions of an almighty and all-powerful God?

The answer is yes. This is the way the Almighty God chose to design the world and to structure our relationship with Him. The correct presumption is that if Esther had not interceded the Jews would have been destroyed. To this day, Jews acknowledge and celebrate this in their annual Feast of Purim. Today's intercessors are just as sure that in many cases without their faithful ministry of intercession God would not have done what He did.

John Wesley is frequently quoted as saying, "God will do nothing on earth except in answer to believing prayer." John Calvin in his *Institutes* affirms that "Words fail to explain how necessary prayer is." He says that the providence of God does not exclude the exercise of human faith. While the Keeper of Israel neither slumbers nor sleeps, Calvin says, "yet He is inactive, as if forgetting us, when He sees us idle and mute."[4]

Today's leaders, from Jack Hayford to Walter Wink, are saying the same thing. Hayford says, "You and I can help decide which of these two things—blessing or cursing—happens on earth. We will determine whether God's goodness is released toward specific situations or whether the power of sin and Satan is permitted to prevail. Prayer is the determining factor."[5]

Walter Wink also rejects the idea that God is the cause of all that happens here on earth. He is omnipotent, but He has also limited His actions on earth in part out of respect for the freedom of His creatures. While affirming that prayer changes us, Wink says, "It also changes what is possible for God."[6]

GOD'S BEST: MOSES AND SAMUEL

If I am not mistaken, the two greatest intercessors in the Old Testament were Moses and Samuel. I surmise this from Jeremiah 15:1 where God says, "Though Moses and Samuel stood before Me, yet My mind could not be favorable toward this people." The main point was that intercessors are not manipulators of God and that some things God has set in concrete. But in order to reinforce the point, God mentions His two best: Moses and Samuel.

I have already mentioned Moses' intercession for Joshua in the battle of Rephidim (Exod. 17). Another even more dramatic example came when Moses went up to Mount Sinai to receive the tables of the law and the people of Israel turned against God and reverted to paganism. God was so angry that He said, "Let Me alone, that My wrath may burn hot against them and I may consume them" (Exod. 32:10). Moses then prayed one of the most touching prayers of intercession recorded in Scripture. As a result, "The Lord relented from the harm which He said He would do to His people" (Exod. 32:14).

Moses' heart was typical of many intercessors I know. At one point he hurt so much for those for whom he was praying that he said to God, "Yet now, if You will forgive their sin—but if not, I pray, blot me out of Your book which You have written" (Exod. 32:32). No wonder God regarded him as one of the best!

An outstanding example of Samuel's intercession came when the Philistines were descending on Israel and Israel was terrified. They said to Samuel, "Do not cease to cry out to the Lord our God for us, that He may save us from the hand of the Philistines" (1 Sam. 7:8). "Then Samuel cried out to the Lord for Israel, and the Lord answered him" (1 Sam. 7:9). The Lord sent thunder upon the Philistines, they became confused, and Israel overcame them.

As did Moses, Samuel showed his intercessor's heart when he later said, "Far be it from me that I should sin against the Lord in ceasing to pray for you" (1 Sam. 12:23). We can be thankful that this is not simply part of ancient history, but that today God has given us many, many of His children with hearts like Moses and Samuel. They are precious gifts to the Body of Christ.

INTERCESSION IN THE NEW TESTAMENT

In the New Testament, Jesus is the intercessor *par excellence*. His prayer for His people in John 17 reveals the loving heart Jesus had for the people and His desire to stand in the gap between them and the Father. To this day He continues to intercede for us. "He ever lives to make intercession for [His people]" (Heb. 7:25).

The theme of this book is not intercession in general, although that is very important. James says, "Confess your [sins] to one another, and pray for one another, that you may be healed" (Jas. 5:16). An excellent book on the subject is Dick Eastman's *Love on Its Knees* (Chosen Books) and there are many others. Here, however, we are focusing on a very specific aspect of intercession, namely intercession on behalf of pastors and other Christian leaders.

John Calvin was not exaggerating when he said that it is almost impossible to explain how necessary prayer really is. Intercessory prayer can be so important that it can save lives.

In Acts 12, Herod decided to placate the Jews in Jerusalem by doing away with some Christian leaders. He specifically put James and Peter on his hit list. He killed James, but he did not kill Peter. We are not told any more details about James's case. But we are specifically told that while Peter was in prison awaiting execution "<u>constant prayer was offered</u> to God for him <u>by the church</u>," (Acts 12:5). As a result, Peter's life was spared, and Herod ended up being eaten by worms (see Acts 12:23). We can safely assume that Peter prayed some himself, but so far as we are informed, the divine power to deliver Peter was released through the intercessors just as the power for Joshua to win his battle was released through Moses.

PAUL'S DESIRE FOR PRAYER PARTNERS

Apparently the apostle Paul knew all about the value of personal intercession for leaders since he requested it five times in his epistles.[7] Let's look at the five texts.

Brethren, pray for us.
1 Thessalonians 5:25

Although "us" is plural, it is likely an editorial plural and Paul is really asking for prayer for himself. In the opening section of his letter to the Thessalonians, Paul assures them that he is praying for them (see 1 Thess. 1:2) and affirming their gifts of faith, hope and love (see 1 Thess. 1:3). At the end of the epistle he asks them to reciprocate, undoubtedly expecting that they will likewise beseech God to increase faith, hope and love in him and his ministry.

Now I beg you, brethren, through the Lord Jesus Christ, and through the love of the Spirit, that you strive together with me in your prayers to God for me.
Romans 15:30

This is a much more specific request for personal intercession, since Paul goes on to ask them to pray that his approaching trip to Jerusalem would be successful and that he would be protected from enemies waiting for him there. He then asks them to pray that he might be able to visit them in Rome. He regards intercession as partnership (striving together) in ministry.

> *You also helping together in prayer for us,*
> *that thanks may be given by many persons on our*
> *behalf for the gift granted to us through many.*
> 2 Corinthians 1:11

As Paul asks the Corinthian believers for intercession, he touches on what Peter also discovered—intercession can be a matter of life and death. In the preceding verses Paul speaks of "the sentence of death" and being "delivered from so great a death." We are not told precisely to what he may be referring, but one possibility would be his stoning in Lystra when he was left as dead. Some feel that he really was dead and that God raised him back to life (see Acts 14:19,20).

> *For I know that this will turn out for my*
> *salvation through your prayer and the supply*
> *of the Spirit of Jesus Christ.*
> Philippians 1:19

Paul writes this request from prison. The word "salvation" in the text means "deliverance," and here Paul is depending on the prayers of others for justice to be done and for him to be released.

> *I trust that through your prayers*
> *I shall be granted to you.*
> Philemon 22

This brief reference could easily be overlooked, but again Paul writes from prison and desires to visit his friend Philemon. He has so much faith that God will answer Philemon's prayers that he asks him to prepare a guest room!

INTERCESSION IS A BIBLICAL CONCEPT

I wrote out these five texts because I feel it is important for us to understand that intercession for leaders, although it may be underutilized today, is a biblical concept. Through intercession, ordinary believers can become a part of the ministry of Christian leaders such as today's apostle Pauls.

As I was writing this chapter I received a phone call from one of my intercessors, Jack McAlister. When I asked him what he had been doing, he said it had been a fairly routine day. He began praying for leaders at 5:30 A.M. and did not finish until almost 8:00 A.M. He said he had been praying for Billy Graham, Bill Bright, me and scores of others. Then he added, "It is so thrilling for me to do this. When I pray for these leaders I participate with them and along with them I receive the blessing of the fruits of their ministry."

This is exactly what the apostle Paul's intercessors were experiencing with him. He writes to the Philippians saying that he was praying for them and "for your fellowship in the gospel from the first day until now" (Phil. 1:5). By "fellowship in the gospel" Paul refers to their partnership with him in his ministry. This is a chief characteristic and reward of intercessors.

INTERCESSION IS SPIRITUAL WARFARE

Jane Anne Pratt is one of Doris's and my personal prayer partners. She is a member of the Dallas, Texas staff of the Eastern European Seminary mission organization. Even before she was a staff member she had been called as a personal intercessor for John Maisel, the mission's president. Jane, I might mention, is a mature, seasoned and experienced intercessor.

In the days soon after the Iron Curtain had come down, John Maisel had made another of his frequent trips to the Eastern bloc. This time he lectured on "Is Jesus God?" at Moscow State University, then to a crowd of 20,000 to 30,000 in Bucharest, then home to their base in Vienna. Jane, in Dallas, was much in prayer for him. The lecture turned out to be excellent and many were saved. Obviously the forces of darkness were greatly upset, not only by Maisel's lecture in Moscow, but by the power channeled through Jane's intercession in Dallas.

What happened shows the degree to which intercession for leaders is in essence spiritual warfare.

On one of those nights at 2:00 A.M., Jane Anne Pratt was awakened by the presence of an incredible force of darkness there in her room. She says, "I battled in prayer and still it was more than I could handle. It drained my whole energy and life support system. I couldn't move—I was totally paralyzed." As she communed with the Holy Spirit she was assured that John himself was in no particular danger at that time. She sensed that "this powerful force of darkness had been sent to destroy John, but it had attacked me because I was standing in the gap." At the peak of the battle, Jane cried out for reinforcements, both angels and intercessors. God sent them both.

In the twinkling of an eye, Jane sensed an angel come into the room and usher out the spirit of darkness. The battle was over but Jane felt limp and drained. Then a fever and laryngitis came. But she rejoiced that the victory had been the Lord's.

The next morning the answering machine in Jane's office recorded a call from Cindy Jacobs who, like Jane, is one of my 19 personal prayer partners. Jane returned her call and routinely asked Cindy how she felt. Cindy's response was unforgettable. "I'm fine, Jane," she said, "but the question is how are you? What was that incredible force of darkness in your room at 2:00 A.M. this morning? That was one of the most powerful principalities I have encountered! I was doing battle with you in intercession until its power was broken!"

Both Jane and Cindy are veteran spiritual warriors. Although the intensity of this battle was unusual, incidents like this are not. As intercessors, they expect frequent bouts with the spirits of wickedness out to destroy the work of God. I agree with Edwin Stube who says, "Intercessory prayer is warfare, and the principal way in which the warfare is carried on. The warfare has to be won first in prayer and then worked out in practice."[8]

PAUL'S PRAYER PARTNERS: EUODIA AND SYNTYCHE

Few commentators have recognized the high probability that Euodia and Syntyche of the church at Philippi were two of Paul's personal prayer partners (see Phil. 4:2,3). Many commentators stress that the women were not getting along well and "possibly they assisted him with material help as Lydia had done some years before."[9] The inference is that, like good women, they perhaps cooked Paul's meals and sewed patches on his garments.

A few commentators do see Euodia and Syntyche playing a much more crucial role in Paul's ministry. F. F. Bruce, for example, points out that the verb for "labored side by side with me in the gospel", is a very strong verb. He says, "Whatever form these two women's collaboration with Paul in his gospel ministry may have taken, it was not confined to making tea for him and his circle—or whatever the first-century counterpart to that activity was."[10]

The verb to which F. F. Bruce refers (*synathleo*) really means that they "contended" or "strived" or "fought at my side." Edmond Hiebert says it "implies united action in the face of opposition and strife" so the metaphor "pictures these women as having served as Paul's fellow soldiers in the battle to establish the gospel in Philippi."[11] This brings us closer to the concept of spiritual warfare. F. W. Beare goes on to argue that these two courageous women were "pitted along with Paul 'against principalities and powers . . . against the spiritual hosts of wickedness in the heavenly places' of Ephesians 6:12, who employ the human opponents of the gospel as their tools."[12]

I quote these recognized biblical scholars not to pretend I am writing an academic monograph, but only to lend some professional credibility to the understanding I have developed of Euodia and Syntyche. I suggest a substantial possibility that Paul is implying these two women "*did spiritual warfare on my behalf.*" If so, they would fit snugly into the profile of personal intercessors or prayer partners I am developing in this book. If nothing else, it helps me suppose that the apostle Paul would understand and approve of what I am trying to say.

■ REFLECTION QUESTIONS ■

1. Talk about the assumption that prayer prevented John Maxwell and Skyline Wesleyan from purchasing the wrong property. Could anyone prove this in a court of law?
2. Review the biblical meaning of "intercession." From your own experience, try to give examples of how intercession has made a difference.
3. The incident of Cindy Jacobs knowing what was happening to Jane Anne Pratt is unusual. Have you ever experienced anything like this?
4. List two or three examples you know about when someone prayed for another person and their prayers were answered.
5. What did Paul mean when he affirms that his prayer partners were doing spiritual warfare on his behalf?

Notes

1. One of Walter Wink's most quoted statements is, "History belongs to the intercessors." The first time I saw it was in his article, "Prayer and the Powers" in *Sojourners*, October 1990, p. 10.

2. Larry Lea's story is related in his book *Could You Not Tarry One Hour?* (Altamonte Springs, FL: Creation House, 1987), pp. 43-46.

3. P. J. Mahoney, "Intercession," *The New Catholic Encyclopedia* (New York, NY: McGraw-Hill Book Company, 1967), p. 566.

4. See John Calvin, *Institutes of the Christian Religion*, Book III:XX:2-3.

5. Jack W. Hayford, *Prayer Is Invading the Impossible* (New York, NY: Ballantine Books, 1983), p. 57.

6. Walter Wink, *Unmasking the Powers* (Philadelphia, PA: Fortress Press, 1986), p. 91.

7. A scholarly, exegetical study of these Pauline requests for personal intercession may be found in Gordon P. Wiles' *Paul's Intercessory Prayers* (Cambridge, England: Cambridge University Press, 1974), pp. 259-296.

8. Edwin B. Stube, *According to the Pattern* (Holy Way, 859 Washington Blvd., Baltimore, MD 21230, 1982), p. 84.

9. Ralph P. Martin, *The Epistle of Paul to the Philippians* (Grand Rapids, MI: Wm. B. Eerdmans Publishing Co., 1959), p. 165.

10. F. F. Bruce, *The Pauline Circle* (Grand Rapids, MI: William B. Eerdmans Publishing Co., 1985), p. 85.

11. D. Edmond Hiebert, *Personalities Around Paul* (Chicago, IL: Moody Press, 1973), p. 166.

12. F. W. Beare, *A Commentary on the Epistle to the Philippians* (London, England: Adam & Charles Black, 1959), p. 145.

The Intercessors

WILFREDO PARETO, THE ITALIAN ECONOMIST, MADE AN amazing discovery around the turn of the last century. He found that, no matter what system of taxation was used by a country, around 20 percent of the people controlled 80 percent of the money. Since then, all kinds of applications of the "Pareto Principle" have been attempted. For example:

- 20 percent of insurance salespeople sell 80 percent of the insurance.

- 20 percent of a book gives you 80 percent of its relevant content.

- 20 percent of the fishers catch 80 percent of the fish.

- 20 percent of church members give 80 percent of the budget.

- 20 percent of the politicians get 80 percent of the votes.

And on and on. Naturally, the 20-80 ratio is a categorical rather than a precise ratio, but the underlying principle holds. It helps us understand the "law of the vital few and the trivial many."

THE VITAL FEW

This 20-80 law can be applied to intercessors in a local church. However, my research shows that more than likely the vital few intercessors are something like 5 percent rather than 20 percent. In other words, 5 percent of the church members in the average congregation provide 80 percent of the meaningful intercession.

I am fully aware that a statement like this can rub some the wrong way for several reasons. Some will say that it *should* not be true and that larger numbers of Christians should do the praying. Others will say that the 95 percent who do only 20 percent of the intercession are not "trivial." I can only agree with the above.

Nevertheless, given appropriate disclaimers, my guess is that it is just as true in your church as it is in mine. Only a rather small number of the church members are recognized by themselves and by others in the congregation as outstanding pray-ers.

The late Waymon Rodgers, who pastored a large church in Kentucky, told the story of a man in his church coming up to him and saying, "I want the keys to the church. I would like to pray in the church." When Rodgers told him that the church was open every day at 8:00 A.M., the man responded, "I used to get up and go to work at 4:30 A.M. Since I have retired, I want to give that time to prayer and fasting." He got the keys and every day that man came to church at 4:00 A.M. and prayed until 7:00 A.M.

As any pastor knows, it would be a big mistake to say to the congregation, "If he can do it, anyone can do it," and attempt to force every church member to pray from 4:00 to 7:00 every morning. It is much more realistic to recognize that man as one of the vital few when it comes to the prayer ministry of the church.

Who are these vital few? They are the people who have the *gift of intercession.*

UNDERSTANDING SPIRITUAL GIFTS

In order to understand the gift of intercession, it is necessary to come to terms with the biblical teaching on spiritual gifts. As Paul says, "Now concerning spiritual gifts, brethren, I do not want you to be ignorant" (1 Cor. 12:1).

The Bible says the church is a body, the Body of Christ (see Eph. 1:22,23). The Body of Christ functions in many respects like a human body. Paul says, "As we have many members in one body, [meaning the human body] but all the members do not have the same function, so we, being many, are one body in Christ" (Rom. 12:4,5). I believe this gives us an important key for understanding what spiritual gifts are and how they work.

If we are all members of the body, how do we know which member we are? How do we know if we are a nose or a toe or a liver or an eyelid? We know by discovering what spiritual gift or gifts we have. "As each one has received a gift, minister it to one another, as good stewards of the manifold grace of God" (1 Pet. 4:10).

God has given one or more spiritual gifts to every believer. No one is left out. Some of our school districts offer special programs for "gifted children." But in our churches the whole program is for gifted children of God because we are all gifted. Not that we have the same gifts. Some are ears and some are eyes, and the ear must not say, "Because I am not an eye, I am not of the body" (1 Cor. 12:16). The better we know our gifts the better we can serve God in our churches.

The Body of Christ is so complex that God wisely does not leave it up to us to choose our own gifts. If He did, too many would decide to be eyes. After all, who would choose to be a liver instead of an eye? But when it comes down to it, the body

---

We don't work for our gifts and receive them as rewards. God graciously and wisely bestows them on us.

---

can live without an eye, but not without a liver. "Those members of the body which seem to be weaker are necessary" (1 Cor. 12:22).

God Selects the Gifts

Only God knows us well enough to decide what part of the Body we should be. The Holy Spirit "distribut[es] to each one individually as He wills" (1 Cor. 12:11). God has set the members in the Body "just as He pleased" (see 1 Cor. 12:11). The gifts we receive come strictly at God's discretion and by His grace. The biblical word most used for spiritual gift, *charisma*, contains the Greek word for grace, *charis*. We don't work for our gifts and receive them as rewards. God graciously and wisely bestows them on us.

What, then, is our individual responsibility? As individual believers one of our highest priorities should be to discover which gifts God has given to us. And then, as we saw, we are to be "good stewards" of them (see 1 Pet. 4:10). We can be good stewards by developing the gifts that we have and then using them in ministry for the glory of God.

How Many Gifts Are There?

A textbook on anatomy would tell us how many parts the human body has. Fortunately, the Body of Christ is not that complex. Differences of opinion exist as to exactly how many spiritual gifts there are. The research I have done and summarized in my book, *Your Spiritual Gifts Can Help Your Church Grow* (Regal Books) leads me to suggest that there are 27, although I have no quarrel at all with others who come up with different numbers.

How do I arrive at 27 gifts?

First, I recognize three major lists of spiritual gifts in the New Testament found in Romans 12, 1 Corinthians 12 and Ephesians 4. None of the three lists is complete in itself—many overlap. Some gifts are mentioned in one list only, some in two, and some in all three. A composite of the 3 lists gives us 20 gifts: prophecy, service, teaching, exhortation, giving, leadership, mercy, wisdom, knowledge, faith, healings, miracles, discerning of spirits, tongues, interpretation of tongues, apostle, helps, administration, evangelist and pastor.

Several gifts are also mentioned apart from the three major lists, five to be exact: celibacy (1 Cor. 7:7), voluntary poverty (1 Cor. 13:3), martyrdom (1 Cor. 13:3), hospitality (1 Pet. 4:9,10) and missionary (Eph. 3:6-9). This gives us a total of 25 gifts indicated as gifts in the New Testament.

Now this next issue is *very important* for understanding the gift of intercession. If none of the 3 major lists of spiritual gifts was complete in itself, and if the composite of the 3 was not complete, could it be that the 25 gifts found in the New Testament could also be an open-ended list and that more could be added? I think it could, although I will be the first to admit I cannot come up with an airtight argument to prove my case. I take some encouragement from the fact that several other scholars and authors have independently drawn the same conclusion. We do it biblically because the Bible does not say the lists are closed, recognizing that an argument from silence proves very little. But we also do it from in-depth observation of how Christians function as members of the Body of Christ.

Some others who follow this line of reasoning suggest 4 gifts, which I do not include in my list of 27, although I have no quarrel with doing so. They are: craftsmanship, preaching, writing and music. I have wished more than once that I had included at least music and made my list 28. Be that as it may, the two gifts I do add to the biblical list are exorcism (which might better be called deliverance) and intercession. A major reason for doing this is that I have seen them in operation.

The Gift of Exorcism

Demonization is now being recognized as a spiritual problem more and more in churches across the theological spectrum. Even in those churches that have had a long ministry history of casting out demons, certain people are regularly called upon for the difficult cases. They have more God-given ability to deal with the demonic than most others do, although I believe that every Christian has been given authority to cast out demons in the name of Jesus.

My wife, Doris, has this gift of exorcism. I clearly recall one Sunday morning in Lake Avenue Congregational Church when Pastor Paul Cedar preached a sermon on healing. Instead of inviting those in need of healing to go to the nearby prayer room after the service as he usually did, he asked those who needed physical healing to come forward. So many responded that the church prayer team was overwhelmed. Cedar then invited people in the congregation who knew how to pray for the sick to come and help, calling Doris and me by name.

I prayed for one woman who had scoliosis, quite a noticeable case of curvature of the spine. The presence of God was strong in the sanctuary, and He moved so powerfully in her back I could feel the vertebrae moving and crunching under my hand as the spine straightened up. As I was finishing I noticed out of the corner of my eye that my friend Phyllis Bennett was patiently waiting for me.

I had known Phyllis and her husband, David, for some time. David was a pastor who had served on our church staff, then pastored some other churches in the area. He performed the wedding for our daughter Karen. At that time he happened to be doing a doctorate at the Fuller School of World Mission where I teach. They had recently spent a few months in India where David was doing his field research.

Phyllis told me she had been suffering from a terrible pain in her chest, which her doctor could not diagnose. Since it had similar symptoms to an ulcer, her doctor had put her on ulcer medication, even though an ulcer had not shown up on the x-ray (20 percent of ulcers go undiagnosed from x-rays). It was not responding well at all to the medical treatment she was receiving. Then she showed me an ugly rash on her left forearm where the flesh had actually begun to fall off in chunks.

As I prayed for Phyllis, I sensed, as I do from time to time, that nothing at all was happening—just the opposite of the previous woman I had prayed for. When I finished, I began giving her some words of consolation and faith, knowing very well that the ulcer was still there. I had not yet noticed that Doris, after praying for another person herself, had come up beside me.

An intense look came on Doris's face and she gently but firmly pushed me to one side. The Spirit of God had indicated to her that she was to take a different approach. She told Phyllis to look into her eyes and almost instantly she locked horns in the unseen world with a demonic spirit that she knew Phyllis had picked up through a curse while in India.

Casting out demons is not the usual Sunday fare in our Congregational church sanctuary on Sunday mornings, but Doris was experienced enough to bind the demon and not allow it to speak or manifest in any way. After a minute or two, Phyllis's eyes opened with a look of terror as if she were watching a horror movie, her body jerked a bit, then total peace. The evil spirit was gone.

The pain in her chest was instantly healed! It left immediately. Phyllis went back to the doctor who took her off the medication. Two weeks later she passed me in her car, rolled down the window, and held out her left arm. The rash was well on its way to recovery. It had been caused by the medication she was taking for the "ulcer."

Now here is the point. I have a spiritual gift of healing and I see quite a few people healed when I pray for them. However, if it had not been for Doris and her spiritual gift of exorcism, Phyllis would likely still have her ulcer. I myself had no sense at all that we were dealing with anything more than a physical ulcer. But this is how the Body of Christ works. "The eye cannot say to the hand, 'I have no need of you'" (1 Cor. 12:21).

Experiences like this encourage me to believe that we do well to add the gift of exorcism to the list of spiritual gifts. I will elaborate on the gift of intercession in some detail, but first we need to understand the differences between spiritual gifts and Christian roles.

GIFTS AND ROLES

Every spiritual gift, like every member of the human body, is itself in the minority. More members of your body are not fingers than are fingers. More are not lungs than are lungs. Likewise in the church. More members are not pastors than pastors. More are not teachers than teachers. More are not healers than healers. And we could go right down the list of gifts in the same way.

Although relatively few Christians have any particular one of the spiritual gifts, all Christians, without exception, have roles that parallel most of the gifts. For example, not all Christians have the *gift* of evangelist, but all have the *role* of being witnesses for Christ and leading people to the Lord. Not all have the *gift* of giving, but all have a *role* of generously giving tithes and offerings. Not all have a *gift* of healing, but all have a *role* of laying on of hands and praying for the sick. Again, we could go right down the rest of the list.

This distinction is extremely important. We all do many, many things in our churches using the multiple roles God has given us. But usually we do a few things with a higher and more consistent degree of power and effectiveness because we receive a special anointing from the Holy Spirit through our spiritual gift or gifts.

Intercession as a Christian Role

Intercession, as I have mentioned, is only one kind of prayer. But it is so important that Jesus Himself is described as an intercessor. Jesus Christ, at the right hand of God, "also makes intercession for us" (Rom. 8:34). Likewise, the Holy Spirit "makes intercession for the saints according to the will of God" (Rom. 8:27). The Father, of course, is not mentioned as an intercessor because He is the One to whom the intercession is made.

On the human level, Paul characterizes himself as an intercessor when he says to the Romans, "Without ceasing I make mention of you always in my prayers" (Rom. 1:9).

Before developing the idea of intercession as a spiritual gift, I want to make it clear that intercession is a *role* expected of every faithful Christian. In fact, I do not know of any Christian brother or sister who does not, on a fairly regular basis, pray for others. Paul says to Timothy: "Therefore I exhort first of all that supplications, prayers, intercessions, and giving of thanks be made for all men" (1 Tim. 2:1). James says, "Confess your trespasses to one another, and pray for one another, that you may be healed" (Jas. 5:16).

Not only should every one of us be interceding for others, but most of us undoubtedly should be doing it much more than we are. If I am honest, I will have to admit that although I do intercede for others, I do not intercede enough. I need to intercede more for my spouse, my children, my extended family, my colleagues in ministry, my pastor and my friends, both saved and unsaved.

At the bare minimum, a decent Christian life should be characterized by at least one designated time each day for prayer, including intercession. How long this daily time should be I will discuss later on. Here my point is simply that the rule is not just for some Christians but for all of them. Intercession is a universal Christian *role.*

Intercession as a Spiritual Gift

Intercession is not one of the 25 spiritual gifts mentioned specifically as gifts in the New Testament. But, like the gift of exorcism, I believe it should be added to the list. When I talk about this to pastors, they almost invariably tell me that in their congregations are certain people whom they and others openly recognize as having a special prayer ministry, over and above that of the average person. This is an early clue that they might have the gift of intercession.

Here is my definition of the gift of intercession:

> The gift of intercession is the special ability that God gives to certain members of the Body of Christ to pray for extended periods of time on a regular basis and see frequent and specific answers to their prayers to a degree much greater than that which is expected of the average Christian.[1]

Those with the gift of intercession:

- Pray longer. One hour a day is the minimum I have found; more frequently they pray two to five hours a day.
- Pray with more intensity.
- Enjoy prayer more and receive more personal satisfaction from their prayer times.
- See more frequent and dramatic answers to their prayers.
- Are acutely aware of hearing quite clearly from God. Many have an accompanying gift of prophecy.

How many members of an average congregation have the gift of intercession? The answer to this question is not fully known. Undoubtedly, further research may turn up some significant variables. Certain denominations or theological traditions may have more active intercessors than others. I say "active" because I am convinced there are many people with the gift of intercession out there in our churches who have not yet discovered their gift or started to use it effectively because their church environment is not conducive to releasing this gift.

One of my prayers is that God will use this book to help change the environment so that multitudes of churches across denominational lines will aggressively encourage the ministry of intercession on all levels.

The figure I previously mentioned in connection with the "law of the vital few," 5 percent of the average congregation having the gift of intercession, seems to be a reasonable working hypothesis. I encourage intercession in my "120 Fellowship" adult Sunday School class. When I did a survey, I found that 7 of my approximately 100 members had the gift of intercession: Cathy Schaller, Lil Walker, Joanna McClure, Mary Stermer, Elizabeth Philip, Mary Wernle and Christy Graham. That came out to 7 percent, slightly higher than my projection.

WOMEN AS INTERCESSORS

It was interesting to discover that all of those with the gift of intercession in my class were women. This is not unusual. I have not as yet done enough research to come up with a firm figure, but my observations over the years lead me to guess that 80 percent of those with the gift of intercession are women, across theological and cultural spectrums.

I have found that certain spiritual gifts seem to be biased by gender. Women tend to show a higher occurrence of the gift of pastor (this does not necessarily relate to ordained ministry, but to pastoral caregiving) and the gift of evangelist. Men tend to show a higher occurrence of the gift of leadership (as in serving as senior pastor of a congregation) and the gift of teacher. The two genders might be more similar in the occurrence of other gifts such as the gift of exhortation or the gift of service, just to offer some concrete examples.

But why would more women be intercessors? Psychological profiles in general have shown women to be more intuitional and men to be more rational. Some intercessors themselves have suggested that a woman's biological function of conception, gestation and the travail of giving birth might have something to do with it. A major ministry of intercessors is to bring into being the purposes of God, and many describe some of their more intense periods of intercession as travail. Mothers know even better than could the apostle Paul the full meaning of his statement, "My little children, for whom I labor in birth again until Christ is formed in you" (Gal. 4:19).

Later on I will sketch a profile of personal intercessors, but meanwhile I think the lyrics of a song entitled "Prayer Warrior" by the outstanding Gospel group, Heirloom, describe them as well as any:

> You may see her in the grocery with her children
> Or in the city nine to five each working day
> She's a mother or a teacher or a woman all alone
> But she's something else entirely when she prays.
>
> We don't see her lonely nights of intercession
> Or the tears she sheds with every whispered prayer
> We may not see the secret things hidden in her heart
> But the eyes of God are watching her with care.
>
> She's a prayer warrior down on her knees
> Wrestling with powers and principalities
> Standing in the gap for others
> For her sisters and her brothers
> Reaching heaven with her heart.[2]

THE OFFICE OF INTERCESSOR

An office in a church goes beyond simply a gift. My understanding of "office" is a public recognition by the Body of Christ that a certain member has a particular spiritual gift and is released to use that gift in regular ministry. This is the foundational principle of what we know as ordination to the ministry.

Conferring an office takes several different forms, anywhere from the public ordination service of a person who will subsequently use the title "Reverend" and receive certain privileges from the denomination and the Internal Revenue Service, to the naming of a person to be a fifth grade Sunday School teacher. Sometimes the person in the office is reimbursed, sometimes the service is voluntary. Either way it has an official recognition.

My suggestion is that churches do something that not many are now doing: Establish an explicit office of intercessor, and give public recognition to those who have the gift of intercession. We do it for those with the gift of pastor, evangelist and teacher. We do it with the gift of mercy (such as minister of visitation), the gift of service (such as deacon or deaconess), the

---

All Christians must fulfill their role as intercessor, but some have a gift and ministry far above the ordinary.

---

gift of exhortation (such as minister of counseling) and many more. I think we should add intercessor to the list.

I am observing that as a part of the great prayer movement now sweeping our nation we are seeing more and more congregations taking intercessors and the office of intercession more seriously than in the past. Some have added a full-time staff member with the title of pastor of prayer or minister of intercession or some other designation. Two current examples in outstanding churches are Bjorn Pedersen who serves under Lutheran pastor Walther Kallestad of the Community Church of Joy in Phoenix, Arizona; and Onie Kittle who serves under pastor Conrad Lowe of the North Parkersburg Baptist Church in Parkersburg, West Virginia. I could mention many more examples.

We need to be sensitive to the fact that not every individual with the gift of intercession will accept the office. This is because with the public recognition comes a higher level of responsibility, accountability and therefore commitment. Some do not desire this. Also, intercessors will be the first to know that in the office they will be subject to a higher intensity of spiritual attack. It is risky to say, "Yes, I have the spiritual gift of intercession and I am prepared to hold myself accountable to the Body of Christ for its use in ministry." But some are willing to take the risk, and as a result awesome new spiritual power is being released in churches and communities across the country.

MINISTRIES OF INTERCESSION

Intercessors in general engage in four specific kinds of ministries.

We will understand this better if we are able to make the biblical distinction between gifts, ministries and activities. In 1 Corinthians 12 we read that there are "diversities of gifts" (v.4), "differences of ministries" (v.5), and "diversities of activities" (v.6), all under the working of the same God.

I take this to mean that different people with the same spiritual gift will have different *ministries* assigned to them by God. For example, among those with the gift of evangelist some may have a ministry of personal evangelism and others may have a ministry of public evangelism.

Other people with the same ministry will have different *activities* assigned to them by God. Take those who have a ministry of public evangelism, for example. Some may be called primarily to do citywide crusades, while others may be called to local church-based evangelism. Of the latter, some may be itinerant, going from church to church and others may be evangelistically gifted pastors who use their gift primarily in one pulpit.

This principle will apply to any spiritual gift, including the gift of intercession. The four ministries most frequently exercised by those with the gift of intercession are general intercession, crisis intercession, personal intercession and warfare intercession. Some intercessors will do all four on a more or less regular basis, while others will specialize in fewer than four, frequently concentrating on only one of the ministries.

1. General Intercession

Those who have a ministry of general intercession will spend long hours praying over prayer lists, prayer guides and any number of miscellaneous prayer requests given to them. Many churches collect slips of paper with prayer requests on Sunday mornings. General intercessors will pray for them during the week. Ask a general intercessor to pray for something and you can rest assured it will be well prayed for.

2. Crisis Intercession

A crisis intercessor prays almost exclusively on assignment, and the assignment comes from the Father. They do not respond well to random requests for prayer from individual people, and most of them would be bored to tears with a prayer list. They like to go into their prayer time with worship and praise, draw near to the Father, and hear directly from Him what they are to pray for. Some assignments are short term, some long term. Once God tells them to pray through a crisis situation they will hang on to it like a bulldog until it is resolved or until God "releases" them from the assignment.

My friend Christy Graham says, "I fit mostly into the category of 'crisis intercessor.' The Lord shows me specific concerns and people for which to intercede. Usually, but not always, it is for a specific time of crisis that I carry the burden to pray." She says that frequently the Lord supernaturally gives specific insight about a particular person's need. She adds, "Along with the information comes a burden to pray and a sense of responsibility."[3]

Among other things, Christy had been given a long-standing

and indefinite assignment to pray for Albania. When I first heard this I felt sorry for poor Christy because there appeared to be no chance whatever that Albania, the world's most anti-Christian nation, would ever open to the gospel. But the world stood in awe as things changed in 1991 and Albania opened. The angels may be rejoicing, but none more than Christy Graham whose prayers, along with those of many others, had a part in opening that nation for God's Kingdom.

As I read Paul's word about Epaphras in Colossians, I have a hunch I am reading about a crisis intercessor. Paul says that Epaphras is "always laboring fervently for you in prayers," and not only does he have a "great zeal" for the Colossian believers, but also for those in Laodicea and Hierapolis (see Col. 4:12,13). That sounds like the kind of assignments intercessors such as Christy Graham receive from God.

3. Personal Intercession

Some intercessors receive a special calling to pray on a regular and intense basis for a specific person or persons. Usually these are pastors and other Christian leaders. This whole book is an in-depth examination of this ministry. Biblically, as I have mentioned previously, I believe Euodia and Syntyche of the Philippian church are two examples of Paul's personal intercessors (see Phil. 4:2,3).

4. Warfare Intercession

Some intercessors are called especially to engage the enemy in high-level spiritual warfare. This is an advanced kind of intercession and by far the most demanding and potentially dangerous of them all. Since many crisis intercessors and personal intercessors find themselves in direct conflict with the forces of darkness from time to time, some may argue against making a separate category for warfare intercession. But I believe there is value in recognizing that some intercessors do this on a much more regular basis than most.

Two excellent sources for more information on strategic-level intercession are Cindy Jacobs' book, *Possessing the Gates of the Enemy* (Chosen Books), and my book, *Warfare Prayer* (Regal Books).

Discovering Your Gift of Intercession

Many at this point will be asking, "I wonder if I might have the gift of intercession?" If you do have it, remember that it is only because God has graciously chosen to give it to you. It is not one of those skills such as ballet dancing or playing baseball that you acquire through hard work and persistence. Since God gives the gift, your responsibility is to discover whether or not you have it.

The process of discovering whether you have the gift of intercession is the same as any of the 26 other spiritual gifts. I have elaborated on this in some detail in my book *Your Spiritual Gifts Can Help Your Church Grow* (Regal Books), so I will only summarize the process here. Here are five steps you need to take to see if you have this or any other gift.

1. Explore the Possibilities

At this point you need to know that the gift of intercession is one of the spiritual gifts God distributes to the Body of Christ. All Christians must fulfill their role as intercessor, but some have a gift and ministry far above the ordinary.

2. Experiment with the Gift

Try intercession as much and in as many ways as you possibly can. This experimentation should be long-term and undertaken in a serious way. Ask God to show you through the process whether you have the gift or whether you do not. If your gift is not intercession, move on and discover what your gift or gifts are. And still be a faithful pray-er.

3. Examine Your Feelings

If you have a gift of intercession, you will grow in your desire to pray. The Bible says, "It is God who works in you both *to will* and to do for His good pleasure" (Phil. 2:13, italics mine). If you find after a period of time that intercession is hard work or drudgery and you do not look forward to doing it, chances are you do not have the gift. But if praying for relatively extended periods of time is your joy and delight, begin to believe you have the gift.

Cindy Jacobs expresses it well. "People who have the gift of intercession," she says, "love to pray. They would rather not do anything else. When people ask me how long I pray in a day, I reply, 'As much as possible!'" When she unplugs her telephone and spends whole days in prayer, "Those days are pure bliss to me!" she says.[4]

4. Evaluate Your Effectiveness

Part and parcel of receiving a spiritual gift is to receive supernatural help from the Holy Spirit to bring about the effectiveness of the ministry. Are you hearing clearly from God? Are your prayers being answered with more than average regularity? Do you sense special power being released through your prayers? If so, you may well have the gift.

5. Expect Confirmation from the Body

I like the story that Graham Fitzpatrick, a confirmed intercessor, tells of how he discovered his gift. He had read about the renowned Father Nash who would intercede for hours for the evangelist Charles Finney. And he found it gave him great peace and joy to picture himself interceding for hours also. But his problem was that he was immature in the things of the Lord and had no way of knowing for sure if this was an inner witness of the Holy Spirit or not. So he asked God to show him.

Sure enough, the Holy Spirit spoke clearly to two other more mature believers about him. According to Graham Fitzpatrick, one man he had just met for the first time "said to me that God wanted me to be an intercessor for other people." Then a woman Fitzpatrick knew, but who was unaware of his yearning for intercession, said that God had given her the same message. Fitzpatrick says, "So God used these two Christians to confirm what I thought was His speaking to me, really was Him and wasn't my own imagination or a demon."[5]

One more thing. If you do discover that you have the gift of intercession, do not be reluctant to acknowledge you have the gift. Do not engage in false humility. You are not "bragging" about being an intercessor any more than Billy Graham is bragging about his being an evangelist or your pastor bragging that he or she is a pastor. The enemy will use your reluctance to let others know you have a gift to neutralize its influence in Christian ministry. It is only part of good stewardship to thank God for the talent He has given you, and use it to bear fruit thirty, sixty and one hundredfold.

▬ REFLECTION QUESTIONS ▬

1. Discuss whether you think it is possible for God to give spiritual gifts to Christians today that are not mentioned as gifts in the New Testament.

2. Explain in your own words the difference between spiritual gifts and Christian roles.

3. Why do you think more women than men have been given the spiritual gift of intercession?

4. Do you know anyone who would fit into one or more of the

four ministries of intercession mentioned in this chapter? Name them and discuss their ministry.

5. Are you one to whom God has given a gift of intercession? Discuss the reasons for your answer.

Notes
1. C. Peter Wagner, *Your Spiritual Gifts Can Help Your Church Grow* (Ventura, CA: Regal Books, 1979), p. 263. See also pp. 74-76.
2. Copyright 1989 by WORD Music (a Div. of WORD Inc.). All Rights Reserved. Used by Permission.
3. Christy Graham, "The Ministry of Intercession," *Body Life* (Newsletter of 120 Fellowship Sunday School Class, Pasadena, California, July 1987), p. 7.
4. Cindy Jacobs, *Possessing the Gates of the Enemy* (Tarrytown, NY: Chosen Books, 1991), p. 71.
5. Graham Fitzpatrick, *How to Recognize God's Voice* (Chichester, England: Sovereign World, 1987), p. 48.

Why Pastors Need Intercession

THREE

I AM CONVINCED THAT MOST CHURCH MEMBERS HAVE LIT-
tle or no appreciation of the cost of being a pastor.
They know what their pastor looks like and sounds
like on the outside, but they have little more idea of
what is happening on the inside than they have about
what is happening on the inside of their digital watch
they look at many times a day.

If God is going to raise up a new army of intercessors who will support pastors and other Christian leaders in effective, fervent prayer, these intercessors need
to know both the scope and the urgency of the task
ahead of them. I am going to be as frank as I possibly
can in this chapter. I do not want to be sensational.

This is not a column for the *National Enquirer*.
Nothing I say about pastors and other leaders is to be
taken as critical any more than a doctor diagnosing hep-
atitis or high blood pressure is critical of the patient.

The purpose is healing. I believe that intercession can not only be therapeutic for pastors' spiritual and emotional maladies, but much more importantly, I believe prayer can be preventative.

PASTORS ARE BEAT UP

The pastor most church members see, know and relate to over a period of time conforms to a well-established social role model. Certain things are expected of a pastor that are not necessarily expected of an automobile mechanic or a lawyer. The title "Reverend" carries strong social connotations.

Church members tend to take this for granted. Not pastors! Pastors are constantly at work projecting a suitable image for a clergy person. They are trained to do this in seminary and Bible school. It does not come naturally.

The pastors church members see week in and week out are on their best behavior. They are appropriately dressed, they have a cheerful disposition, they are affirming, they do not lose their temper, they watch their language, they treat their spouses well, they are unselfish, they work hard, they keep smiling and they hope their people see them as Christlike. But this is only part of the story.

Pastors are also human beings. They are saved by grace, but they are saved and sanctified no differently from the auto mechanics and lawyers in their congregations. Many, if not most, pastors will actually remind their people of this in their sermons from time to time.

When pastors talk about a certain temptation, for example, they might say, "I am not exempting myself. I am human. This is as much of a temptation for me as it is for you." The people usually acknowledge this as an honest appraisal. But they do not really believe it, mainly because they do not want to. Part of their own Christian well-being depends to a degree on following a pastoral leader whom they regard as somewhat higher on the scale of piety and spiritual attainment than they might ever be. Using society's help, they often put their pastor on a spiritual pedestal.

Pastors are also trained not to be hypocrites. They know very well they are not all their congregations expect them to be. Their spouses know this also, but few others do. Consequently, pastors are caught in a bind, for they sense God's calling on their lives to be a pastor and they know that they cannot do an effective job as a pastor if they do not outwardly conform to their congregation's expectations. But how do they handle what is going on inside?

In a word—pastors need help—at least more help than they have been getting. In the course of a year, I meet and interact with hundreds of pastors. Even though I do not relate to them as a counselor or a pastor to pastors, I find that many are beat up; spiritually, emotionally and sometimes physically.

Where can they go for help? They are reluctant to go to any of their church members, for the word could too easily leak out: Our pastor is failing us by not conforming to our expectations. Pastors in the same denomination are usually on friendly terms with each other but somewhat distrustful at the deeper levels. What would church members think if their pastor was seeing a professional counselor? Pastors of other churches in the same community are likely prospects for help but frequently overburdened and unavailable. Beyond those circles, most pastors simply run out of meaningful relationships.

Happily, there are some exceptions. A fair number of pastors do not fit this rather bleak picture I am painting. They have little internal conflict because deep down they actually are what they are expected to be emotionally and spiritually. Some are not, but they have found sources of help and are managing their situation well. I wish I could report that these are in the majority but I am afraid I cannot. Without wanting to oversimplify a terribly complex situation, I do want to point out that

Satan has many pastors just where he wants them. They are vulnerable to his attacks.

OUR EPIDEMIC OF FALLING PASTORS

Over the past couple of decades, an alarming number of pastors have dropped out of the ministry for two main reasons: pastoral burnout and sexual immorality. The numbers have reached epidemic proportions.

I cannot remember hearing about pastoral burnout 20 years ago. It must have existed, but not to the degree we see it today. The situation I have described, resulting in pastors being so beat up, makes it quite easy to understand why so much burnout would occur. The enemy knows this well and has become quite astute at raising frustrations through feelings of inadequacy, hypocrisy, guilt and low self-esteem to such levels that selling insurance can seem to some a more attractive way to make a living.

A good bit of psychological research is currently being done on causes and remedies for pastoral burnout. Good time-management training is helping many to avoid it. Nevertheless, if I am correct in suspecting that the powers of darkness are also at work in causing burnout, spiritual weapons are also needed. This is where intercession for pastors has enormous potential.

PASTORAL INDISCRETION

Satan wins significant battles through causing pastoral burnout, but he inflicts immeasurably more damage to the cause of Christ when he influences a pastor to fall through sexual immorality.

Before I go into more detail on this delicate subject, let me just remind us that most American pastors have not nor will they ever fall into sexual immorality while they are in the ministry. In fact 8 out of 10 have had no overt problems in this area, which by comparison is only half of the number of other church members who have had similar problems. How many have gone all the way? A survey by the clergy journal *Leadership* found that 12 percent of pastors had actually committed adultery.[1] This means 88 percent have not.

The enemy knows pastors are beat up; he knows they are vulnerable, and he attacks them at their weakest point.

Surveys like this would never have been dreamed of a generation ago. Elmer Gantry was not looked upon as a realistic prototype of anything but a miniscule fringe of American clergy. Now the picture has changed. I have been dropping news items in a file folder I never looked back into until now. I am appalled. I count 26 media reports of sexual immorality on the part of high-profile clergy; almost half of whom I know personally.

A front-page article in the *Los Angeles Times* carries the headline, "Sex Abuse Cases Rock the Clergy: Disclosures of misconduct—a problem hidden for years—are on the rise." A nationally syndicated column by the Associated Press announces that "Sex scandals in higher ranks shake up hierarchies."

Evangelicals, charismatics, fundamentalists, Pentecostals, liberals, Roman Catholics all wish they could point their fingers at the others, but none is exempt. Here is a mainline bishop, known widely as an "evangelical." Here is a seminary professor. Here is a televangelist. Here is a civil rights folk hero. Here is a megachurch pastor. Here is a best-selling author. Here is a missions leader. Here is a liberation theologian. Here is a black, there is a white. Here is a 25-year-old, there is a 60-year-old. Here is a pastor from Massachusetts, there is a pastor from Arizona. Where is it going to stop?

Reporting this makes me angry! I am not angry at my friends who have fallen even though I, along with the rest of the Body of Christ, have been harmed. I am angry at the enemy who, I feel, is getting away with far too much these days. We often fail to recognize the depth of the spiritual battle we are fighting.

The enemy knows pastors are beat up; he knows they are vulnerable, and he attacks them at their weakest point. This is not to say those who have fallen are not themselves guilty and do not have character flaws that need to be repaired through humility, repentance, reconciliation, restoration and holiness. But I do hope and pray we will learn how to use our spiritual weapons more effectively in putting a stop to these blatant and all too successful attacks of the devil.

PASTORS NEED INTERCESSION

Every Christian needs intercession. The little girl in the sixth grade learning what AIDS means needs intercession. The long-haul truck driver trying to witness to his friends about Jesus Christ needs intercession. The Christian stock broker wrestling with the ethics of that last deal needs intercession. The mother and homemaker raising a family of four needs intercession. I do not want to ignore the need for more consistent ministries of intercession across the board.

But I do want to argue that pastors and other Christian leaders need intercession more than ordinary members of the Body of Christ. This may sound strange and even arrogant at first, but let me propose five reasons why I believe it to be true.

1. Pastors Have More Responsibility and Accountability
Most of us Christian leaders get chills up and down our spines

when we read James 3:1, "My brethren, let not many of you become teachers, knowing that we shall receive a stricter judgment."

All Christians will come before the judgment seat of Christ, but pastors and other leaders have been forewarned that there is a divine double standard. One for "teachers" and one for all the rest.

In other words, in the eyes of God a given sin is worse for a pastor to commit than for others. The first problem, of course, is the sin itself and that may be the same for everyone. But the second problem is the violation of the *office*, which is even more serious. When an office such as pastor or teacher (including seminary professor) has been granted by God and recognized by the Christian community, it is a grievous offense to break that trust.

Accepting a position of leadership in the Christian world is running a risk. Sin becomes more dangerous than ever before. And this is one reason why pastors have a greater need for intercession.

2. Pastors Are More Subject to Temptation

Make no mistake about it, the higher up you go on the ladder of Christian leadership, the higher you go on Satan's hit list. The devil is characterized as a roaring lion seeking whom he may devour. If he has a choice, he will devour a leader before he will devour anyone else. And he will use every weapon in his arsenal to do it.

Satan uses the *world* (Eph. 2:1,2). He tempts pastors with greed and power and pride. Money and power team up with sex as some of the strongest lures for ministers. It took recent investigative reporting by the secular media to uncover some of the greed among Christian leaders, which others of us have not particularly wanted to face. And I believe more such news is to come. The love of money is the root of evil, and Satan has been getting in at that point more than some have suspected.

Satan uses the *flesh* (Eph. 2:2,3). Enough has been said about illicit sex. Satan also perverts the mind with pornography. Other ministers are tempted to fall into gluttony or alcohol and substance abuse.

Satan also uses *"the devil"* (1 Pet. 5:8; cf. John 13:27). This means demonization, spells, curses and incantations. To imagine that pastors are only subject to the world and the flesh, but not the devil, is in itself a clear satanic deception.

It is true that all Christians are subject to all of the above. But Satan is more specific, persistent and intentional when it comes to pastors and other leaders.

3. Pastors Are More Targeted by Spiritual Warfare

It has now become known that over the last several years satanists, witches, New Agers, occult practitioners, shamans, spiritists and other servants of darkness have entered into an evil covenant to pray to Satan for the breakdown of marriages of pastors and Christian leaders. The spiritual warfare has intensified.

In my book, *Warfare Prayer* (Regal Books), I distinguish three levels of spiritual warfare: (1) Ground-level spiritual warfare, which is ordinary deliverance ministry; (2) Occult-level spiritual warfare, which involves spells and curses by spiritual practitioners of darkness; and (3) Strategic-level spiritual warfare, which deals with territorial principalities and powers. All three levels interact with each other to varying degrees, but the warfare is different in each case. Here I am dealing with the middle- or occult-level of spiritual warfare. Special kinds of intercessors, particularly the warfare intercessors I mentioned in the last chapter, are needed to deal with this most effectively. And other intercessors are needed as a backup.

Spiritual warfare is such an important issue that I want to

be sure we do not just think it is a figment of someone's imagination. I have personal correspondence from two respected Christian leaders who have had firsthand exposure to this. They help us understand the reality of the struggle we have been drawn into.

The first report is from John Vaughan of the International Mega-Church Research Center and Southwest Baptist University, Bolivar, Missouri. I have known and respected John for years. Among many other things, he is the editor of the *Journal of the North American Society for Church Growth*. The scenario of this report is an airplane flight from Detroit to Boston where Vaughan was to do a pastors' seminar.

John had not conversed or paid much attention to the man in the seat next to him until he saw the man bow his head and move his lips as if praying. When he finished John said, "Are you a Christian?" The man had no way of knowing that Vaughan himself was a Christian, a Baptist pastor and a university professor.

He seemed shocked by the question and said, "Oh, no. You have me all wrong. I'm not a Christian, I'm actually a satanist!"

John asked him what he was praying for as a satanist. He said, "Do you really want to know?"

When John said he did, the satanist replied, "My primary attention is directed toward the fall of Christian pastors and their families living in New England." He asked John what he was going to do in Boston.

John reports, "After a brief conversation about my ministry and its purposes for the Kingdom of God, he indicated that he needed to return to his work!"

John Vaughan says that encounter made him realize just how essential intercession for pastors really is. Did Christians take time to pray for their pastors in New England that day? Whose prayer was answered—the Christian's or the satanist's?

Award-winning satanists. Bill McRae is the chancellor of two prestigious evangelical institutions near Toronto, Canada—Ontario Bible College and Ontario Theological Seminary. Previously he pastored the North Park Community Chapel in London, Ontario.

He reports that while he was a pastor, "It was brought to our attention that a group of satanists who worshipped in a church situation within London had committed themselves to pray to Satan for the elimination of a number of our evangelical leaders in the city through marriage and family breakdown. During that summer the cell group in London was honored at a particular satanist convention for being so effective and successful during that year."

Why did they win the award? McRae says, "In the course of the previous year they had succeeded through their prayers to Satan to eliminate five of our very significant leading men from pastoral ministries through immorality and marriage breakdown!"

Bill McRae says that he was very deeply involved with one of the pastors who was going through this nightmarish and disgraceful fall from Christian ministry. He says, "We were very much aware of the desperate need for prayer, but I must frankly confess none of us was quite as alert to the reality of the satanic warfare we were fighting until it was all over."

McRae also tells of a group of his friends who went into a restaurant in London and observed a prayer meeting in a corner booth. They introduced themselves as fellow Christians, but the pray-ers quickly identified themselves as members of the church of Satan in London. They admitted (bragged?) that they had been praying that night specifically to Satan for the destruction of a certain pastor. McRae says, "They mentioned his name, and he is a very good friend of mine in one of the leading churches in London. It once again brought home to me the dark reality of the satanic battle in which we are engaged."

Keith Bentson, a veteran missionary to Argentina, reports

about spiritual warfare from San Juan, Argentina. San Juan, he says, is a particularly strong center for the occult. The evangelical work is not growing in that city. Keith says, "I have heard of five pastors who, within the last two or three years, have been involved in immorality, with the consequence that there are many, many Christians around the city who do not attend any church, having lost confidence in their spiritual leaders."

Spirits of lust. Some of the closest contact I have with pastors comes during the two-week Doctor of Ministry courses I teach twice a year. In a recent course, I said something that

---

Pastors need intercession more than other Christians because by the very nature of their ministry they have more influence on others.

---

sounded humorous when it came out of my mouth. Here I had 50 pastors from across the denominational spectrum and from many different parts of the country. It was an advanced course, so they had all studied with me before and knew me. On the first day of class I told them, as I usually do, that their two weeks would not only be a time of learning new material, but that God would also use it as an opportunity for the pastors to minister to one another and draw closer to God.

Then I mentioned that my wife, Doris, who is also my secretary and to whom many of them had talked on the phone, has had a powerful ministry of praying for pastors one-on-one and has helped them a great deal. I casually told them that she has a particularly effective track record of delivering pastors from demonic spirits of lust. Then I said, "So if any of you have a problem with lust, go see my wife!"

I said it so spontaneously and naively that we all burst out in laughter. But then what happened? No fewer than six of them made appointments with Doris for deliverance sessions! They went home with a new lease on life. Several wrote back or called telling Doris how different and more enjoyable life has been since they were delivered from those foul spirits. One wrote, "For the first time since we have been married, my wife and I can now pray together."

Nothing said here should cause us to suppose that demonization relieves pastors or others of moral responsibility. The roots of the activity of a spirit of lust, more often than not can be traced to the "lusts of the flesh" (see 1 John 2:16) or sin that needs to be identified and dealt with biblically. Part and parcel of the deliverance process is typically (1) a personal recognition of and hatred for the sin; (2) a sincere desire to get rid of it; (3) a courageous first step of faith—e.g. making an appointment to see Doris; and (4) confession of the sin, frequently in considerable detail.

This fulfills James 5:16: "Confess your trespasses to one another, and pray for one another, that you may be healed." In this case the healing is spiritual. Upon sincere repentance, the root sin is forgiven by God's grace and the legal grounds of the subsequent demonic activity are effectively removed. Once this is accomplished, the demonic spirit can be cast out relatively easily. Without sincere humility and repentance, the demon either stays or soon returns with reinforcements.

I have dealt with this subject of spiritual warfare in quite some detail for two reasons: First, I want to make sure we understand that it is real. It is certainly not the only cause, but I would not be surprised if it were a major cause of so many pastors falling into sexual immorality.

Second, I want us to understand that there is a remedy, namely the power of God released through effective, intelligent intercession in the name of Jesus. My burden in this book is to explain in all detail possible how this power can be released for repairing the damage already done by the enemy and preventing future occurrences.

4. Pastors Have More Influence on Others

The fourth reason why pastors need intercession more than other Christians is that by the very nature of their ministry they have more influence on others. If a pastor falls, more people are hurt and set back in their spiritual lives than if others fall. The ripple effect is incredibly devastating. Strong Christians are crushed by the hypocrisy and betrayal they feel. Weak Christians take the pastor's behavior as a license for them to do likewise.

Not only does the fall of a pastor injure an untold number of people, but it also directly influences churches. My interest in church growth always focuses strongly on the pastor because we have evidence that the pastor is the major institutional factor for determining the growth or nongrowth of a local church. Satan hates churches that glorify God and extend God's Kingdom, and he does what he can to bring them down. No wonder he focuses his sights on pastors.

But in the plan of God the gates of hell will not prevail against the advance of the Church (see Matt. 16:18). Intercession for pastors is one important ingredient to release God's plan for the Church's fullest implementation.

5. Pastors Have More Visibility

Because pastors are up front, they are constantly subject to gossip and criticism. When church members have Sunday dinner, the pastor and the sermon of the morning are frequent topics of conversation. People talk about the good and also the bad. The pastor is closely observed and it is no secret. Just knowing this places a difficult burden on pastors and they need supernatural help to handle that situation well. Intercession opens the way for them to receive this help.

INTERCESSION IMPROVES MINISTRY

It is not a simple matter to conduct the type of research that proves or disproves the power of prayer. However, Nancy Pfaff, an intercessor, church growth consultant and founder of Nevada Church Growth has attempted it. She designed a research instrument as a project in graduate school and surveyed 130 pastors, evangelists and missionaries. Intercessors trained through Iverna Tompkins Ministries of Scottsdale, Arizona, agreed to pray 15 minutes a day for one of the 130 leaders over an entire year.

About 89 percent of those surveyed indicated that the prayer had caused a positive change in their ministry effectiveness. They reported more effectiveness in the use of their particular spiritual gifts, a higher level of positive response to their ministry, more discernment and wisdom from God, increased wholeness and completeness in Christ, improved attitudes, more evidence of the fruit of the Spirit, better personal prayer lives and heightened leadership skills.

Pfaff's research also uncovered some important variables. She found that daily prayer for leaders was more effective than weekly or monthly prayer. Also, persistent prayer was shown to be important. She reports, "Where intercessors stopped praying for their assigned leader after a few weeks, the leaders indicated no significant positive change in their lives and ministries during that year."[2]

Intercession also seems to help church growth. Nancy Pfaff found that of 109 pastors covered by intercessory prayer, 60 percent indicated concomitant growth of their churches. A pastor from Pennsylvania testifies, for example, that in the 12-month prayer experiment period his church grew from 15 to more than 600. No wonder Pfaff says, "There exists a tremendous reservoir of untapped prayer power in every church which can be affirmed, trained, and deployed to see the lost won, the apathetic revived, the 'backslider' restored, and the committed made more effective."[3]

Back when the well-known Evangelism Explosion program was moving out from Coral Ridge Presbyterian Church in Fort Lauderdale, Florida, and spreading across the country, Archie Parrish, who was then serving as director, made an important discovery. Even though the program was working well, he introduced a new innovation. He had each participating church enlist two church members who were not in the Evangelism Explosion program to pray for each Evangelism Explosion worker, especially on the Tuesday nights when the program was in operation. The evangelist was responsible to report back to his or her two intercessors each week. When intercessors prayed, the number of professions of faith in cooperating churches doubled!

Pastors and other Christian leaders are needy people. But they are God's chosen ones to move His Kingdom forward. Faithful and intelligent intercession can release them to be all God wants them to be.

■ REFLECTION QUESTIONS ■

1. This chapter suggests that pastors are "beat up." Why do you think this could be true? Give examples.
2. What is it that makes a pastor more responsible for moral behavior than the average Christian?
3. Distinguish between the three levels of spiritual warfare mentioned in this chapter, giving examples of each from your knowledge or experience.
4. Discuss the possibility of evil spirits causing lust in a pastor's life. Does this relieve the pastor of moral responsibility?
5. If intercession will improve your pastor's ministry, what suggestions could you make to release more prayer on your pastor's behalf?

Notes
1. *Leadership* editors, "How Common Is Pastoral Indiscretion?" *Leadership*, Winter Quarter 1988, pp. 12,13. The "8 out of 10" is my extrapolation from the data reported.
2. Nancy Pfaff, "Christian Leadership Attributes Dynamic Increase in Effectiveness to the Work of Intercessors," *Journal of the North American Society for Church Growth*, 1990 edition, p. 82.
3. Ibid., p. 83.

Secrets of Pastors' Prayer Lives

IN ADMIRABLE TRANSPARENCY, BAPTIST PASTOR MARK LIT-
tleton says, "Parishioners would never dream it, but
there is a segment of the ecclesiastical nobility—
myself included—for whom personal worship (aka
'devotions,' 'quiet time,' 'QT') has been a struggle. First,
it's finding the minutes. Those phone calls in the morning always seem to foul up your communion with God.
Or maybe it's the kids. Or the sweet smell of coffee from
the kitchen."[1]

Many church members take for granted that their
pastor, as their spiritual leader, spends considerable quality time alone with God on a regular basis. They love
their church and they love their pastor and they assume
that their pastor is a "man of God" or a "woman of God."
Little do they know that one of the higher items on the
list of pastoral frustrations is the gap between the prayer

life that pastors know they need and desire to have, but cannot seem to make happen in real life.

One pastor says, "Like most busy people I am plagued by pressures, deadlines, phone calls, 'emergencies,' and on and on. Sometimes I think the devil works overtime just to keep me from prayer." Knowing what I know about the devil, I think the last sentence could be a severe understatement.

How Much Do Pastors Pray?

Several surveys have been done on the prayer life of pastors. Before I report on them, however, I want to be sure that you realize I may not be talking about your pastor when I cite averages. Your pastor might be one of those above average, even far above average. Chances are that you do not really know offhand where your pastor stands because few church members do. Not that your pastor *intends* that his or her prayer life be kept a secret, but in most cases it is.

When *Leadership* journal conducted a survey of 125 pastors' prayer lives, the majority felt they were virtually without human support in their devotional lives. By some mutual agreement, it seems to be an inappropriate topic of conversation in the parish.

One of the pastors surveyed says, "I get the feeling others don't think my personal devotional life is important." In the years that he had been on the staff of this particular church, he says, "Not one person (including the senior pastor) has asked me about the health of my personal faith. I feel totally unsupported in this aspect of my life."[2] The majority of the 125 pastors surveyed harbored similar feelings.

I personally conducted a survey of 572 American pastors across regional, age and denominational lines. I wanted to find out just how much time a day pastors spend in actual prayer. In this survey I was not counting Bible study, reading devotional books, listening to worship tapes or other components of a fully rounded devotional life. I was dealing only with prayer. In my sample I found:

- 57 percent pray less than 20 minutes a day.
- 34 percent pray between 20 minutes and 1 hour a day.
- 9 percent pray 1 hour or more a day.
- The average prayer time was 22 minutes daily.

I did not find a significant variation in age, although the pastors over 60 years of age seemed to pray a little less than the others. I found no regional variation. I did find what may be a significant theological variation in that pastors who perceive themselves as Pentecostals/charismatics report praying for longer periods of time than those who see themselves as evangelicals or liberals. I will get back to this later on when I discuss the issue of prayer and church growth.

The *Leadership* survey to which I referred, also found that pastors pray 22 minutes a day by and large, so this figure seems to be consistent. But my survey also showed that 28 percent—more than 1 out of 4—prayed less than 10 minutes a day!

What can we compare this to? The Gallup Poll found that 88 percent of Americans pray to God. Of those who do pray, 51 percent of them pray every day. But it did not report the amount of time.

CLERGY PRAYER IN OTHER NATIONS

I personally conducted similar surveys in four other nations. I found that:

- Australian pastors average 23 minutes a day in prayer.
- New Zealand pastors average 30 minutes a day.
- Japanese pastors average 44 minutes a day.
- Korean pastors average 90 minutes a day.

In Korea, another survey showed that 83 percent of pastors across denominational lines pray one hour or more a day. One out of three prays two hours or more. One of my close friends, Pastor Sundo Kim, whose Kwang Lim Methodist Church is reported to be the largest Methodist church in the world (more than 50,000 members in 1990), has a prayer closet built into his study. It contains a pillow on the floor for kneeling, a Bible on a low stand, a cross and a picture or two on the wall, and nothing else. He told me he spends at least an hour and a half a day in that closet.

That hour and a half is over and above the hour or more he spends every single day leading his church's predawn prayer meeting and the time he spends in groups and in one-on-one praying during the day. Like many other Korean pastors, Kim also has a motel-like bedroom and bath connected to his study because he ordinarily spends all of Saturday night there fasting and praying for Sunday's ministry. His prayer habits are about average for Korean pastors.

Do Pastors Pray Enough?

In recent years, I have been spending a good bit of time in teaching pastors on the subject of prayer. Whenever I bring up the subject, they frankly admit to me and to each other that they know their prayer lives are not all they should be. Although some have first-rate personal prayer habits, and some are happy with their 22 minutes a day, the great majority are not.

Pastor Mark Littleton remarks that he does his best to stick to a consistent prayer life, "through sick and sin." His exasperation surfaces when he says, "You try it with the television on. With the television off. At home. At your office. Under the beech trees in the park. In bed. Out of bed. You go for a week straight and don't miss once. The next week you miss seven for seven."[3]

Books and sermons on prayer feature a standard list of

heroes of the faith who have had extraordinary prayer lives. John Wesley rose at 4:00 each morning and spent two hours a day in prayer. Martin Luther said, "I have so much to do today, I will have to spend the first three hours in prayer, or the devil will get the victory." Adoniram Judson disciplined himself to withdraw by himself and pray seven times each day. John Welch of Scotland, the companion of John Knox, committed 8 to 10 hours a day to prayer.

John Hyde of India prayed so much that he earned the nickname, "Praying Hyde." Henry Martyn, David Brainerd, George

---

Prayer is the chief way we express our love to God and the chief way we receive God's love for us.

Muller, Robert Murray McCheyne, Hudson Taylor, George Fox and a few others habitually make this all-star list. All of these spiritual giants accomplished great things for God, things which most of today's pastors would love to duplicate. But if their performance in ministry depends on sustaining that kind of a prayer life, most pastors I know simply despair.

No one says it better than Mark Littleton. He says reading about these superpray-ers "nearly wipes you out." "As holy as David Brainerd was," Littleton says, "you get a bit tired of him lying in the snow, praying for six hours, and getting up wet. Not from the snow, though. From the sweat!"[4]

Richard Foster speaks for me as well as for many others when he says, "Many of us are discouraged rather than challenged by such examples."[5] I can still remember reading the biography of Praying Hyde when I was a young Christian. I was so discouraged when I finished that I think it was the last Christian biography I ever read!

Enough lamenting about the current state of affairs. Few will deny that pastors and other Christian leaders in general need better prayer lives. The question now is what to do about it. I think the answer is twofold:

- First, pastors need to pray more.
- Second, pastors need to learn to receive intercession.

I will elaborate some on the first part of the solution here, then use the rest of the book to deal with the second part.

PASTORS NEED TO PRAY MORE

One of the reasons I am not going to deal with many of the whys and hows of praying more is that by far the greatest majority of books on prayer deal with this. We do not lack resources. The average Christian bookstore's section on prayer contains many excellent titles. True, these may not be specifically aimed at the prayer life of the pastor, but the general principles of a disciplined and rewarding prayer life apply across the board.

As I peruse the literature, however, I feel that four issues are worthwhile mentioning because they are dealt with either not at all or, in my opinion, inadequately. I refer to (1) the issue of time, (2) the issue of gift projection, (3) the issue of church growth and (4) the issue of personal ministry.

THE ISSUE OF TIME

How much time should be spent in prayer? How important is the time factor?

A fruitful way to approach the answer to these questions is

to explore the essence of prayer. When all the trimmings are peeled away, prayer must be seen basically as a relationship. It is our individual, personal relationship with God the Father. The way for this to happen was provided by Jesus Christ on the cross. He shed His blood for the remission of sin, the sin that separates us from God. Through Jesus, our sin is forgiven and our fellowship with God is restored. Then, and only then, does prayer take its true form. We now love God because He first loved us and paid the price to bring us to Himself.

Prayer is the chief way we express our love to God and the chief way we receive God's love for us. It is the most exquisite expression of our personal relationship. If we can understand that through prayer our divine love affair with the Father is cultivated, we can more accurately assess the value of time in prayer. All we know about human love relationships tells us that clock time together is essential if the relationship is to grow.

The Minimum Daily Requirement

For one thing, prayer time must be regular. A consensus among Christian leaders who have specialized in matters of prayer, devotional life, spirituality and Christian discipleship is that there should be a time of prayer every day. No pastor should let a single day go by without a specific time set aside from other activities for talking to God.

I believe it is helpful to develop habits of praying while we are taking a shower, driving a car, standing in line, riding a bus or washing the dishes. But when I speak of a daily prayer time, I mean programming blocks of time for God on our calendars and Day-Timers. Not a day should go by without prayer on any Christian's schedule, but especially on a pastor's schedule.

To imagine that on some days our schedule is too busy to fit in time with God is to make a decision with fairly deep implications. No one has any more time than anyone else—24 hours a day. How each of us decides to use that time boils down to our personal priorities. Pastors in general have more ultimate control over their daily schedules than the majority of humans who work in other professions.

I realize that some pastors feel their schedule controls them, but this is due to faulty time management, not the nature of the pastoral vocation. This means that if we feel we cannot schedule a daily time with God, we need to admit that our relationship to God is not one of our highest personal priorities. If this is true, spiritual disaster could be right around the corner.

Not long ago I was conversing with a friend about our families. He said, "After years of marriage there are things you begin to take for granted. For instance, I don't tell my wife I love her every day—she knows it and has known it for years." I did not feel it was appropriate to reply at that moment, but in my mind I was saying, "I do!"

Even though my wife and I have been married more than 40 years, I try to tell her explicitly at least once every day that I love her. In my mind, some things are too important to take for granted such as my love relationship with my wife and my love relationship with God. I intentionally try to keep them among my highest priorities.

I imagine some may be saying we should not be so legalistic. God is a God of grace, not law, and He will maintain the relationship with us on His initiative whether or not we perform by scheduling an intentional daily prayer time. I have to agree with a theology of the grace of God, and chronic legalism is not a characteristic of my personal Christian life-style. But I will say that on this particular issue of time with God, if I err I would far rather err on the side of legalism than on the side of excessive leniency.

I again like the way Mark Littleton puts it, "I have to ask myself the question," he says, "Are all the activities that scream for my time and attention in twentieth-century America really essential? Am I missing the burning bush for trying to keep the lawn cut?"[6]

Time Must Be Sufficient

Having a regular daily prayer time is the first and most essential component of a pastor's personal prayer life. A second important consideration is the amount of time spent in each prayer session. I personally find myself less legalistic about the time factor, although I can quite confidently state that as a general principle *the more time spent daily in prayer the better.*

I have found that almost all pastors I know who have a true heart for deepening their personal relationship to God agree with this. The arguments I have heard against it cause me to be suspicious of their proponents. They too often sound like rationalizations designed to justify a slipshod devotional life that has become a life-style.

What are the time ranges? The 22-minute-a-day average should probably be considered the minimum in our particular (non-Korean!) cultural context. John Welch's eight hours or Luther's three hours or Wesley's two hours a day are probably far beyond any realistic proposal for today's American pastors.

As a starter, I would recommend that if you are praying less than 22 minutes a day, you make that your first goal. Then where do we go from there?

I have been strongly influenced by Larry Lea's book *Could You Not Tarry One Hour?* (Creation House). I think Lea has been a principal contextualizer of the Korean prayer movement into our American society. He makes a compelling case for aiming toward one hour a day.

Another authority on intercession from whom I have learned a great deal is Pastor Mike Bickle of the Metro Vineyard Fellowship of Kansas City. Mike agrees with Larry Lea on the one hour a day. The *Leadership* survey of 125 pastors that I have previously cited asked them: "How much time per day do you think you *should* spend in prayer?" More than half (53 percent) said 30 to 60 minutes and about half of the others (24 percent) said more than 1 hour.[7]

In the light of this survey, I suggest pastors and other Christian leaders agree that a minimum of 22 minutes, pushing for 1 hour a day, be our norm for daily prayer time.

But what about the *quality* of our time with God? Isn't quality more important than quantity?

My suggestion is: It is more advisable to start with quantity than quality in daily prayer time. First, program the time. The quality will usually follow. Mike Bickle says that when you first spend 60 minutes in a prayer time do not be surprised if you come out of it with only 5 minutes you consider quality time. Keep it up and those 5 minutes will become 15, then 30, then more. The ideal, of course, is to end up with both quantity and quality, not one or the other.

Our society, a generation that has combined two working parents, high divorce rates, and single-parent families, has reduced the quantity of time parents spend with their children. To compensate, they have developed a concept of "quality time" with the kids. Psychological studies on the children have now shown that no "quality" of time can substitute for quantity of time with the children. One of the high priorities of these children who are now becoming parents themselves is to return to a life-style in which they can spend "quantity time" with their children. I believe the same principle applies to our time with our heavenly Father.

THE ISSUE OF GIFT PROJECTION

I purposely do not say much about the syndrome of gift projection in my seminars or my classes; mainly because it is frequently painful for some leaders to discover they are unintentionally involved in it. I dealt with it in my book *Your Spiritual*

Gifts Can Help Your Church Grow (Regal Books) and many readers have commented that it was one of the most helpful sections for them. It helped them get rid of some false guilt complexes they had developed.

As I was in the process of researching for this book, I felt I heard God saying quite clearly to me that I was to include a brief section on gift projection here also. I am praying that what I have to say about relating gift projection to intercessory prayer will not be offensive to any other leaders who have been teaching on prayer and intercession; although I know up front that it will run against the grain of some of the things they have been teaching. On the other side, I also know it will free up many people to be what God wants them to be instead of what they perceive other people want them to be.

What is gift projection?

Some people who customarily minister powerfully in a certain area because they have been given the spiritual gifts to do so, do not realize that the power they regularly see in their ministry is being released through a *charisma* or spiritual gift. It does not occur to them that although God has chosen to give them this particular gift, the same God has also chosen to give different gifts to other members of the Body of Christ.

Much of this lack of understanding is rooted in the notion, held by many classical Pentecostals and others, that all the spiritual gifts are given to all believers who have been duly filled with the Holy Spirit. Some of them also limit the number of spiritual gifts to the 9 found in 1 Corinthians 12 rather than regarding the whole list of 27 I mentioned in chapter 2 as legitimate spiritual gifts. This starting point quite easily leads to gift projection.

Inflicting False Guilt

The message that often comes through is, "I am an ordinary Christian just like you are. God has not given me any special privileges. What He is doing through me, He also wants to do through you. If you really want to, you can do the same powerful ministry I do because Jesus is the same yesterday, today and forever. I urge you, along with other Christians, to make up your mind to do whatever is necessary so that with the help of God you can also do the ministry I am doing."

The unintended result of projecting spiritual gifts on others who have been given different gifts is false guilt, discouragement and frustration. The guilt is false because people who do not have the particular spiritual gift try to do what the gifted ones do, and find they cannot. So where do they assign the blame?

- Am I not spiritual enough?
- Do I have unconfessed sin?
- Am I unworthy of God's love?
- Is God mad at me?
- Don't I pray enough?
- If only I was as consecrated to God as this spiritual giant I am listening to, I would be able to match their effectiveness in ministry!

I will refrain from mentioning people's names at this point. But I could give names that are household words in the Christian community of those who regularly project the gift of evangelism, the gift of hospitality, the gift of healing, the gift of word of knowledge, the gift of discernment of spirits, the gift of mercy, the gift of faith, the missionary gift and many others.

Another frequent projection is the gift of intercession, and that is why I have brought up the subject. The historical heroes of the faith such as Praying Hyde, John Welch, David Brainerd and Adoniram Judson obviously had the spiritual gift of intercession. But so does this particular pastor of our own generation who tells of spending three to five hours each day in prayer and whom I have heard say in public, "If Reverend so-and-so prayed as much as I do each day, his church would be as large as mine!"

Those with the gift of intercession who urge others to be more like them would do well to review Paul's teaching in 1 Corinthians 12—14. Do all have gifts of healing? Obviously not. Do all work miracles? Obviously not. Do all have a gift of

---

A central purpose in the Kingdom of God is the multiplication and growth of Christian churches, and we know that prayer is a chief instrument for releasing God's purposes into reality.

---

administration? Obviously not. Do all have the gift of helps? Obviously not. Do all have a gift of intercession? Obviously not. (See 1 Corinthians 12:27-30.) If we all had one gift, including the gift of intercession, the body would turn out to be an eye. The apostle Paul says, "If the whole body were an eye, where would be the hearing?...But now God has set the members, each one of them, in the body just as He pleased" (1 Cor. 12:17,18).

I will repeat what I said in chapter 2. Although God has given the gift of intercession to some and not to others according to His plan, He has given every one of us the *role* of prayer and intercession. We all must be pray-ers and growing in our prayer life. Few pastors have the gift of intercession and can be expected to pray two to five hours a day as intercessors do. But all have a *role* of prayer and intercession and by using the role they can and should pray between 22 minutes and 1 hour a day without feeling guilty about not praying more.

THE ISSUE OF CHURCH GROWTH

The direct relationship between prayer and the growth or non-growth of churches is not yet known. Much is known about the indirect relationship because Jesus said, "I will build my church," and He has been doing just that for almost 2,000 years. A central purpose in the Kingdom of God is the multiplication and growth of Christian churches, and we know that prayer is a chief instrument for releasing God's purposes into reality. No doubt it is due in part to prayer that we are seeing such extraordinary church growth in many parts of the world these days.

Nevertheless, not much in the literature on prayer or the literature on church growth shows how the connection is actually made, and particularly what strategies we can develop to see the power of prayer help churches grow faster than they already are in a given time and place. Some of the experiments we have conducted in Argentina were reported in my first book in this "Prayer Warrior" series, *Warfare Prayer* (Regal Books). Through them we have begun to see that strategic-level intercession and spiritual warfare can help churches grow. I hope to go into considerably more detail on the matter in the fourth book of this series.

Meanwhile, the survey of 572 American pastors I have mentioned gave us not what I could call scientific conclusions, but at least they were clues. When we look out on today's world we are immediately impressed that by far the most massive growth of churches is found within the Pentecostal/charismatic traditions. Statistics provided by David Barrett indicate the following:

- In 1965 there were 50 million Pentecostals/charismatics.
- In 1975 there were 96 million.
- In 1985 there were 247 million.
- In 1991 there were 392 million.

Although I do not pretend to be a professional historian, I think the following statement would be correct: *In all human history there has never been a nonpolitical, nonmilitaristic, voluntary human movement that has grown as rapidly as the Pentecostal/charismatic movement has grown in the last 30 years.*

Take just one denomination, the Assemblies of God. Although the denomination had existed for several decades previously, its vigorous worldwide growth began only after World War II. In the last 40 years or so it has already grown to become the largest or second largest denomination in more than 30 nations of the world. In one city alone, São Paulo, Brazil, there are 2,400 Assembly of God churches!

In almost any large metropolitan area of the world where there is an openness to Christianity and to new churches, the largest churches are usually Pentecostal or charismatic. I have a list of the 20 churches of the world that have a membership of more than 20,000 each. Of those churches, 14 are Pentecostal or charismatic.[8]

How does this relate to my survey? As I previously mentioned, the one significant variable I found in the amount of time American pastors spend in prayer had to do with the Pentecostal/charismatic pastors. When broken down by theological traditions we saw the following:

- Liberal pastors average 18 minutes a day.
- Evangelical pastors average 17 minutes a day.
- Pentecostal/charismatic pastors average 46 minutes a day.

America is one of the nations where the Pentecostal/charismatic churches are outgrowing all the others by leaps and bounds. This, of course, does not necessarily apply to individual churches as such, but to the general overall statistics. Could the fact that the pastors of those churches set aside more than twice the amount of time for daily prayer than do the pastors of slower growing churches have anything to do with their vigorous rate of growth?

If so, it may point to another benefit that could be received under the blessing of God as pastors begin pushing those 22 minutes toward 1 hour.

THE ISSUE OF PERSONAL MINISTRY

I am praying that this chapter, which has been very frank and honest, will be used by God to draw thousands of pastors closer to Him than they have been before. I am confident He will do that.

A word of encouragement along these lines came from a pastor I had lunch with soon after I did the survey. He shared that the most significant part of our conversation for him was discovering what I was learning about prayer. He writes, "After hearing about the average time in prayer for pastors as 22 minutes, and what God is doing in response to the prayers of His people around the world, I have determined to spend two hours a day in prayer." Since beginning this, he says, "I have sensed the presence and power of the Holy Spirit in a new way in my life and ministry."

Most pastors I know recognize that they need to improve their prayer lives. One way they can do this is to personally pray more regularly, and for longer periods of time. They can also learn to receive the intercession of others. The rest of the book will deal with receiving personal intercession.

As pastors and leaders we tend to be activists. We can easily identify with Joshua out there in the battle of Rephidim. What we need to learn more about is how God can bring into our lives and ministries people who, as Moses did for Joshua, will spend hours and days in the presence of God on our behalf so that His power flows liberally to give us the effectiveness we desire in our personal ministry.

▬ REFLECTION QUESTIONS ▬

1. Does it come as a shock to discover than even pastors have a difficult time maintaining a quality prayer life? Why?
2. Do you think it is too legalistic to suggest that ordinary Christians find a specific time each and every day to pray?
3. How do you feel about the suggestion that the first step in improving one's prayer life is to concentrate on the quantity of time, assuming that quality will eventually follow?
4. "Gift projection" is a rather difficult concept to grasp. Discuss it until you feel you understand it. Why is it dangerous?
5. Do you know how much your pastor prays each day? Do you feel it should be considered private information? Why?

Notes
1. Mark K. Littleton, "Some Quiet Confessions About Quiet Time," *Leadership*, Fall Quarter, 1983, p. 81.
2. Terry C. Muck, "10 Questions About the Devotional Life," *Leadership*, Winter Quarter, 1982, p. 37.
3. Littleton, "Some Quiet Confessions," p. 81.
4. Ibid.
5. Richard J. Foster, *Celebration of Discipline* (San Francisco, CA: Harper & Row Publishers, 1988), p. 35.
6. Littleton, "Some Quiet Confessions," p. 82.
7. Muck, "10 Questions," p. 34.
8. For more detail on the growth of Pentecostal/charismatic churches see Stanley M. Burgess and Gary B. McGee, eds., *Dictionary of Pentecostal and Charismatic Movements* (Grand Rapids, MI: Zondervan Publishing House, 1988), pp. 180-195; 810-829.

Receiving Personal Intercession

FIVE

THE STATEMENT I AM ABOUT TO MAKE SOUNDS PUZZLING at first.

My personal prayer life is first class! My personal prayer habits are mediocre.

The puzzle, of course, is how can I have it both ways? How can I have mediocre personal prayer habits and still have a first-class prayer life?

My answer is straightforward: I have learned how to receive personal intercession.

MEDIOCRE PRAYER HABITS?

When I say that my personal prayer habits are mediocre, at least I can say they are now better than they used to be.

I did not grow up in a Christian home where church, Sunday School, prayer and the Bible were a normal part of life. It was after I left home that I was born again and became a committed Christian. Some of my early Christian training came through InterVarsity Christian Fellowship where I learned that part of the expected behavior pattern of a Christian was to have a daily "quiet time." They explained to me what it was and I began to do it. Because I have always been able to exercise considerable self-discipline, I maintained a quiet time for years "through sick and sin" as Mark Littleton would say. Throughout seminary and my three terms on the mission field in Bolivia, I had a quiet time day in and day out.

If anyone had asked me at one of those moments when I was in a particularly transparent mood, I would have admitted that I did the quiet time thing pure and simple because it was my duty. I also brushed my teeth, took my vitamins, got my hair cut and changed my underwear regularly. It was part of what respectable Christians did. Although I cannot recall any special good feeling while I was doing it, it did feel good because I had done it.

Then at 40 years of age I went through a mid-career change from a field missionary in Bolivia to a seminary professor in Pasadena, California. It was probably also a mid-life crisis of sorts, although I am not much for self-administered psycho-analysis. But part of what I went through was one day, after being back in the United States for a couple of years, I decided to drop the quiet time. It had become so dry and routine that I reasoned I would be better off without it. So for a number of years I just got up, had my breakfast, and went to work without blocking off any of the time for God I advocated so strongly in the last chapter.

Bad choice! As the next few years went by, I became more and more convinced and convicted that I was not better off without a regular prayer time. My classes were going well, my ministry was fairly well received, and my career was advancing satisfactorily. But I always seemed to be in the midst of unusual amounts of turmoil and polemics. Moving forward was a constant uphill struggle. I began to suffer from high blood pressure and constant headaches. Because I was only marginally in touch with the Lord, I did not have the spiritual insight to realize I had fallen into the habit of doing a great deal in the flesh rather than in the Spirit.

I am sure it was the persistent gentle prodding of the Holy Spirit that began to bring me to my senses and realize I did need to go back to a regular daily time with God. But knowing I was supposed to do it, and actually doing it were two different things. I wanted to start something new, but I also did not want to fall back into the dry routine I had pushed myself through for years.

THE *READER'S DIGEST* SERMON

My pastor, Paul Cedar, came to the rescue. One Sunday morning in the early 1980s, he told the congregation he was going to do something he had never done before and probably would not do again. As a part of his morning message on prayer, he was going to read word-for-word an entire article from *The Reader's Digest.* Sure enough, it was an article on spending time each day with God.

I am sure that many others among the 2,000 in the congregation were touched by the *Reader's Digest* sermon, but none more than I. I knew God was speaking to me, but my chief worry was still how I was going to implement what I knew I had to do sooner or later. At the end of the sermon, Paul Cedar did an enormous favor for me.

Paul said, "I know that some of you have not been having a regular quiet time, and my prayer is that you will start up this week. I'm not going to ask for a show of hands, but I am going to ask that in your heart you make a promise to me as your pastor. I'm going to ask you to promise me you will give five minutes a day to God starting this week."

Five minutes? I honestly do not know what I would have done if he had said 30 minutes or an hour, but I said in my heart, "Pastor Paul, I can handle five minutes a day. You have my promise that I will do it!"

And I did. The next morning I spent five very special minutes with God. The 5 soon became 10. Then 15. The time kept increasing and increasing. Then it plateaued—at about 22 minutes a day! That was before I had done the survey mentioned in the last chapter and found that 22 minutes was the average. The 22 minutes might not be much, but it is a whole lot better than zero.

TARRYING ONE HOUR

I was rolling along at about 22 minutes of prayer a day when I started researching prayer in 1987. One of the early books I read was Larry Lea's *Could You Not Tarry One Hour?* (Creation House). In it he makes such a persuasive case for praying one hour a day, I resolved I would set that as my goal. Now, 3 or 4 years later, I can say I have left the 22 minutes behind; I am peaking more than 30 minutes most days and often more than 40. But one hour? It is still a life goal, and I may make it some day. One hour is a long time for prayer!

I will never forget the first time I ever prayed for one hour. This was back in the 1970s when I was in my prayerless period. I had been going to Korea from time to time to research church growth, and had become personal friends with Paul Yonggi Cho, pastor of the Yoido Full Gospel Church, the world's largest congregation. On one visit, Cho offered to take me to the famous Yoido Church Prayer Mountain.

Because I had never visited the prayer mountain, I jumped at the chance, looking forward to a personal tour. When we arrived, I was wondering how the tour would begin. But Cho, of all things, said, "Now, let's pray!" Pray? I preferred walking around and taking pictures of Prayer Mountain, but naturally I did not express my surprise. Then he said, "We don't have very much time. Let's pray this afternoon only for one hour!"

I wanted to be a good sport, so I sat there on the floor of the huge chapel (Korean style) and started to pray. I prayed a long time. Then I looked at my watch. I thought my watch had stopped! That was one of the longest hours I can remember spending. Time went faster when my wife was in labor!

But Larry Lea seemed to know I needed special help to extend my prayer time. He makes a suggestion (which I have since discovered has a long history in Christian tradition) of structuring our personal prayer times around the Lord's Prayer. This works well for me, for when you *pray* the Lord's Prayer, instead of simply *saying* the Lord's Prayer, you have a ready-made structure to cover everything you possibly need to pray about at one time.

Structure is important to me because I have a very systematic mind. When I pray, my chief distraction is not sleep as I know it is for some others. I am not usually a sleepy person. Just the opposite. My chief distraction is a wandering mind. While I am meant to be praying I will suddenly realize I am far offtrack. I can sometimes rationalize this by supposing it is a track God wants me to be on at the moment, but this does not always work.

I recall one morning while in prayer I found myself replaying the Los Angeles Lakers' basketball game I had watched on television the night before. And I knew that could not be God—the Lakers had lost! Seriously, when my mind does wander, the Lord's Prayer structure helps me know exactly to pick up where I inadvertently left off.

So much for my mediocre personal prayer habits. I am trying, and I know God will help me get better. But meanwhile, I still affirm that I have a first class prayer life because I add to my personal prayer the prayer of my intercessors. I actually believe that the prayers of my intercessors are a real and vital part of my personal prayer life.

DISCOVERING INTERCESSION

I began to discover the power of personal intercession soon after I started teaching my Sunday School class, the 120 Fellowship of Lake Avenue Congregational Church in 1982. This was not premeditated, but rather the spiritual chemistry of the situation.

I had never doubted the authority of Scripture, therefore I never really doubted the power of prayer. Only after the first months of the new class had turned into years did I begin to understand what was happening. For the first time I could recall, I was in the midst of a group of people who were supporting me and my ministry through powerful intercessory prayer.

Not that others who had supported us on the mission field and elsewhere were not praying Christians. But some of those I was now associated with had a contact with the invisible world I knew little about.

I began to get clues when a new pattern formed. On an infrequent but fairly regular basis, people would approach me in pastors' seminars I was doing across the country and say words to this effect: "I heard you x number of years ago, and I'm now hearing you again. Your ministry has an obvious depth and quality that it didn't have before. What is it?"

At first I shrugged off the comments as frivolous. But I began hearing it enough to make me do some evaluation. Sure enough, I was finding an increased spiritual power in my teaching. I had logged enough experience with audiences to realize that what I was saying was moving people in a more profound way. And, strangely enough, much of the content itself was not that different from a few years ago.

I did not realize it was intercession at first, but then I fell into a pattern of reporting the results of my previous week's ministry to the class on Sunday morning and asking them to pray for the following week. Many in the class were so touched by what God had done through me during the week, I realized they were considering my ministry as their ministry also. They were laughing when I laughed and crying when I cried because through their faithful intercession on my behalf, they were doing the ministry with me.

Soon I learned how to answer the question when people asked me why my ministry had improved. "I attribute it to the power of prayer through those who are interceding for me," I would reply.

This was the beginning of experiencing the power and effects of personal intercession, which later led me into full-scale research of the biblical, theological and practical theories that would explain why it is true.

PERSONAL INTERCESSION IS BIBLICAL

In chapter 1, I attempted to make a biblical case for personal intercession. I do not intend to duplicate that here, but I will briefly review a few of the points. Moses praying for Joshua as he fought and won the battle of Rephidim is a beautiful model. The apostle Paul asks for personal intercession for himself and his ministry at least five times. Euodia and Syntyche were in all likelihood two of Paul's personal prayer partners.

Herod decided to kill both James and Peter. He killed James but not Peter and we are told that "constant prayer was offered to God for him by the church" (Acts 12:5). The praying was done in the home of Mary, the mother of Mark, and I would not be surprised if Mary was one of Peter's personal prayer partners.

PERSONAL INTERCESSION IS UNDERUTILIZED

In a brochure written to stimulate prayer for missionaries, veteran missionary Robert Bowers, a medical doctor serving with SIM International, describes this all-too-familiar scenario:

> "Please pray for us," a furloughing missionary says as he leaves a pleasant dinner.
> "We will, we will," his host responds warmly.

Bowers' comment is that this is a bit like saying hello and good-bye—a formality that carries little real meaning. On the surface, a verbal contract was made that this Christian family would pray for the missionary. Their names were probably entered on the list of those who receive the missionary's "prayer letter."

But if this family was typical of thousands of others, the actual amount of powerful, effective intercession invested over that next four-year-term of service was practically nil. Missionaries, pastors, teachers, denominational executives and other Christian leaders affirm the importance of prayer, but lack the know-how to actually make it happen.

As I said on the first page of chapter 1: *The most underutilized source of spiritual power in our churches today is intercession for Christian leaders.*

Fortunately, we are not starting from ground zero. Many outstanding leaders today understand and receive personal intercession. And some important people from the past report the power of intercession in their lives.

One of today's recognized prayer leaders and students of prayer, Armin Gesswein, tells me in a recent letter about Frank

Mangs, perhaps the greatest of the Scandinavian evangelists. Every morning Mangs would earnestly pray to the Lord, "Bless my intercessors today." Then Gesswein, who moves constantly among those who pray, says, "I never hear that from preachers today." I believe Armin has put his finger on a real problem.

We can go back to the eighth century. Boniface, that stalwart missionary to the pagan peoples of Germany, writes to the abbot of a monastery: "We entreat the piety of your brotherli-

---

No question exists in the minds of those who have experienced it; committed, faithful intercession brings increased spiritual power to Christian ministries.

---

ness that we may be helped by your devout petitions...that the few seeds scattered in the furrows may spring up and multiply." And to an archbishop: "We entreat your clemency, that your piety would pray for us in our labors and dangers."[1] Boniface apparently understood this power.

Charles G. Finney, one of the most effective evangelists of the last century, met Daniel Nash early in his ministry. Nash became Finney's personal intercessor and would frequently travel with him and pray while Finney preached. Known as "Father Nash," he gained a reputation for praying long and very loudly. It was said that when he prayed in the woods his voice could be heard throughout the surrounding countryside.[2]

To get more up to date, visitors to the museum in the Billy Graham Center on the campus of Wheaton College in Illinois will see a picture of one of Billy Graham's prayer partners, Pearl Goode. Graham himself attributes much of the evangelistic power of his ministry to Pearl Goode's faithful intercession.

No question exists in the minds of those who have experienced it; committed, faithful intercession brings increased spiritual power to Christian ministries. Why is it, then, that so few ministers utilize it? I believe there are five important reasons for this.

1. Ignorance

I have no doubt that ignorance is the number one culprit for our lack of plugging in to personal intercession. The great majority of Christian leaders just have not thought about it. Although it is nothing new either biblically or historically, it is simply absent from the day-by-day thought patterns of most Christian leaders.

The thing that made me realize what a role ignorance plays in determining personal intercession was the disproportionate response I began getting when I started to mention this casually in some of my church growth seminars.

While I was developing the seed thoughts for the contents of this book, I would test the waters by using 10 or 15 minutes of a two-day seminar reporting what I was learning. An unusual number of pastors would get back to me saying that what I shared about personal intercession was more important to them than the whole rest of the seminar.

I would receive letter after letter like this one from a pastor in Upland, California: "Following your exhortation on personal intercession, I now have 7 prayer partners praying for me daily. I am seeing a difference in my life! Thank you." I realized that more than anything else, I was rolling back a cloud of ignorance.

In order to illustrate the wide scope of our ignorance as a Christian community on the power of personal intercession, I want to pick up once again on the current epidemic of pastors and other leaders falling into sexual immorality. The scandals have become so widespread and so public that several Christian authors have been researching and writing on the subject. I have made a personal collection of this material because I began to notice a trend reflecting our ignorance of the power of personal intercession.

I will need to mention the names of some of these authors because their own stature and integrity in the Christian community is important for my point. But I want my motive to be fully understood: in no way am I *criticizing* these authors, many of whom are personal friends of mine. I am simply citing them because they represent all of us collectively on this issue. They represent my own state of mind during most of my ordained ministry as well.

Intercession is not thought of. One of the Christian classics of our generation is Richard J. Foster's *Celebration of Discipline* (Harper and Row). He is known as a top leader of the spirituality movement beginning in the late 1970s. He is a man of prayer. When the Jim Bakker affair became public, *Charisma* magazine asked Richard to examine the PTL crisis and analyze it. His resulting article is called "The PTL Scandal." After analyzing what happened, Foster suggests four ways to prevent such things in the future. Not one of the four is prayer![3]

Pastor and radio personality Richard Exley wrote a book, *Perils of Power: Immorality in the Ministry* (Harrison House). It contains no section on prayer or personal intercession. Likewise the book by the famous Christian psychologist, Clyde M. Narramore, *Why a Christian Leader May Fall* (Crossway Books). The same for the late charismatic leader, Don Basham, whose book is titled, *Lead Us Not into Temptation: Confronting Immorality in Ministry* (Chosen Books).

The two major interdenominational clergy journals in the United States each ran an issue on the subject. Here is the *Leadership* journal of Winter 1988 on the general theme: Sex. It carries articles such as "How Common Is Pastoral Indiscretion?" "Private Sins of Public Ministry," "The War Within Continues,"

"Counselling the Seductive Female," "After the Affair: A Wife's Story," "Preaching on That Oh-So-Delicate Subject" and "Treating Casualties of the Revolution."

Among the better known authors are David Semands, Arch Hart, Bill Hybels and Chuck Smith, leaders of peerless wisdom and integrity. I could not find in all of this material a single mention of prayer as a preventative. In the same *Leadership* journal, Randy Alcorn wrote an article, "Strategies to Keep from Falling," suggesting nine preventative measures, none of which is receiving personal intercession.

Ministries Today, the second most influential clergy journal, dedicates a large part of its July/August 1990 issue to "Restoring Fallen Leaders." Some of its articles: "The Restoration of David Alsobrook," "Restoration by Grace," "Pastor—and Addict," "Restoring Fallen Leaders," "Picking Up After an Affair," "If Ministers Fall Can They Be Restored?" and "When a Leader Falls." In this issue the power of prayer is mentioned twice, but both times in the context of picking up the pieces *after* the tragedy rather than for *preventing* the fall altogether.

I was happy to see that Gordon MacDonald's book, *Rebuilding Your Broken World*, does have a section on prayer. He suggests seven "Personal Defense Initiatives (PDIs)." He lists PDI #2 as "Pay the Price of Regular Spiritual Discipline," by which he means, "The cultivation of Scripture study, intercession, meditation, and the general reading on spiritual subjects."[4] However, he does not go on to mention receiving spiritual power through the intercession of others.

To summarize, it does not seem to occur to these leaders, whose stature is so widely respected, to advocate personal intercession as one of the means for preventing pastors from falling into sexual immorality. Why? It apparently simply never occurred to them. This is what I mean when I say that ignorance is the number one reason why we have not been using personal intercession as we should.

2. Rugged Individualism

Cultural anthropologists continually remind us Americans that we are some of the most individualistic people in the world. Many trace it to our frontier mind-set. We are one of the few cultures in the world, for example, where young people leave home, select a mate, and then inform their parents. It would be fully expected that the notion, "If I'm going to get anywhere in life, I'm going to have to pull myself up by my own boot-straps," would also carry over into our spiritual lives. This is known to be true, and to one degree or another we all partic-ipate in it.

The good news is that our individualism encourages us to accept personal responsibility for a given task. The bad news is that we tend to ignore or despise other members of the Body of Christ whom we desperately need. We hate to admit that we need help or that our performance is dependent on other brothers and sisters in Christ.

I will illustrate this by using Jimmy Swaggart as an example. It is not my usual habit to bring up names of leaders who have had severe problems, but this case has been public for so long on national and international media that it is safe to assume I am not telling stories out of school. Furthermore, mutual friends have assured me that Jimmy Swaggart would not object to reit-erating the lesson he himself said he learned for the benefit of the rest of the Body of Christ. I pray this is true because he needs no more personal pain inflicted at this point in time.

First of all, it is important to know something of Jimmy Swaggart's personal prayer life. He says that the Holy Spirit "impressed upon me to give a tenth of my time in prayer and in study of the Word (I don't mean studying for sermons). That amounts to about two and a half hours a day."[5] Swaggart admits that some days he had a hard time keeping to it, but he nevertheless has felt a heavier anointing since setting apart this much time. This calculates to better than 6 times the average pastor's prayer time of 22 minutes.

So apparently Swaggart had a far better than average personal prayer life. Obviously, however, it was not enough to keep him from falling into sexual immorality.

E. M. Bounds says, "The preacher must pray; the preacher must be prayed for." Jimmy Swaggart covered the first part of the formula. It was weakness in the second part that he himself cites as a source of his trouble. How do we know this?

Do it yourself spirituality. Before the scandal had broken in 1988, Swaggart wrote an article for his magazine, *The Evangelist*, titled "The Lord of Breaking Through." The magazine had been printed and mailed before the news became public, so although the article was written previously it was not delivered to our homes until a week after we all knew about his problem. Of course Swaggart knew what he had been doing when he wrote the article, and it sounds to me as if he were trying to deal with his spiritual condition. In the article he says:

> I have always taken pride in my spiritual strength. I have believed that in my relationship with God, if He promised me something, I could have it. I can't recall, in all of my life, ever going to *anybody* and asking them for help.

He does mention that he constantly asks people to pray for him, but this is in the sense of the missionary leaving the home after dinner and asking the host family to pray for him. Then Swaggart goes on to say, quite transparently:

> We are discussing personal weaknesses. Frances said to me one day, "The reason you have such difficulty in such and such an area is because of pride." That

brought me up with a start. I hadn't thought about it, but I had to admit she was right.[6]

Behind this was rugged individualism that did not feel a need for anyone's help. Swaggart was evidently beginning to admit his shortcomings when the scandal broke. Then he went on national television and made his tearful confession. Among other things he said:

> Maybe Jimmy Swaggart has tried to live his entire life as though he were not human. And I have thought that with the Lord, knowing that He is omnipotent and omniscient, that there was nothing I could not do— and I emphasize with His help and guidance.

Again, this is asserting the rugged individualism in which all of us Americans are involved sometimes more than we know. But it is specifically applied to Christian ministry. Then comes the heart of the lesson learned:

> I think this is the reason (in my limited knowledge) that I did not find the victory I sought because I did not seek the help of my brothers and my sisters in the Lord...If I had sought the help of those that loved me, with their added strength, I look back now and know that the victory would have been mine.[7]

I could not agree more. I see personal intercession as a vital activator of the immune system of the Body of Christ. To the degree that we can get rid of the idea, "If I am going to make it with God, I'm going to have to do it myself" we will free ourselves to look elsewhere in the Body of Christ for the God-given resources we so desperately need. Releasing God's power through intercession will go a long way toward preventing the enemy from bringing us down.

And others are now learning the lesson. One of Swaggart's close personal friends, missionary Mark Buntain, wrote an open letter to him after the scandal became public. In it Buntain confesses, "I never once prayed for your own life to be protected from the onslaught of Satan's power...Oh, why was I not pleading with the Holy Spirit to not only anoint you with preaching power, but that He would keep you with His inward power?"

Buntain all but shoulders the responsibility for Swaggart's fall. He says to Swaggart, "I am guilty. I have failed you and failed you badly." Some will say he overreacts, and perhaps he does. But his message is one we all should hear clearly. Serious intercession could have and probably would have changed this low point of contemporary Christian history.

3. Fear
The third reason why personal intercession is underutilized is fear.

There is some justification for the fear some pastors have of personal intercession. They may not have thought it through in detail, but intuitively pastors realize that when they begin to relate to personal intercessors they move into a deeper level of vulnerability and accountability than before. This is not just imagination; it is a fact. Personal prayer partners make your life become much more of an open book.

I have mentioned that John Maxwell of Skyline Wesleyan Church has a team of 100 men who are committed to intercede for him and his ministry. I have visited the church several times and know some of his prayer partners personally. One of them is Dick Hausam who has received a special assignment from God to focus his prayers on John's moral life. John is on the road about as much as an NBA basketball player. He is no more exempt from temptation as any other man in his 40s. But almost every Sunday, Dick will approach John and say, "How did it go this week?" John replies, "It went real well, but I don't know how it would have gone if you hadn't prayed for me."

This is what I mean by vulnerability and accountability. I realize that not every pastor is up to this, and fortunately such a degree of transparency is not a prerequisite for relating to personal prayer partners. Most prayer partner relationships start with much less personal accessibility. Some grow into it and some do not. But even those that do not are much better than no prayer partners at all.

Another justification for fear emerges from a characteristic of prayer partners, particularly those with the gift of intercession. They frequently receive information directly from the Lord about the pastor or leader.

Experienced and discerning intercessors can be expected to know things about the pastor's life that the pastor supposes are secret. Fortunately, God does not entrust such information to intercessors unless He is sure their level of maturity and wisdom can handle it. My own prayer partners and others I know who pray for other leaders tell me that God shows them things they are not at liberty to share with the pastors they are praying for.

We really should not be afraid of this because the intercessors have been given the information not to harm us personally or to harm our ministry, but just the opposite. Through their prayers, obstacles to the productivity of our ministry and to our personal fulfillment in Christ are removed, and we are more liberated than we have been.

4. Spiritual Arrogance

I wish spiritual arrogance were a minor issue, but I am afraid it is not. For many pastors it is a principal obstruction to their being open for personal intercession.

I learned about spiritual arrogance from Pastor Paul Walker

of Mount Paran Church of God in Atlanta, Georgia. I have known Paul for years and greatly admire him. Not only is he a minister of the classical Pentecostal tradition, but he holds a Ph.D. degree in counseling. At this writing his church is one of the most attended churches in the nation.

Paul Walker told me the story of a problem that had arisen with a prominent leader in his church. Walker felt God was directing him to purchase a second campus for his church; a large Baptist church with a modern sanctuary seating around 3,000. This particular church had been closed for eight years. The purchase of the property, refurbishing and necessary additions were going to cost $10 million, and it would open the overcrowded Mount Paran to a new phase of growth by using the two campuses simultaneously. But the prominent church leader wanted nothing of it.

The situation escalated until it became critical. The leader's sphere of influence with a rather vocal core developed negativism. The whole church could have been affected to the point of creating divisiveness. It was all the more difficult because Paul and the church leader had been close friends for 25 years. Paul said to me, "I guess all it takes is a difference of opinion on future ministry to put a long-term friendship on the skids!"

Paul Walker is in a personal relationship with about 50 intercessors in his church. Among other things, these people are in regular communication with him. It is a well-known fact that trying to get a telephone call through to a megachurch pastor in the United States is almost as difficult as getting one through to the President in the White House. But Walker has given instructions to his office staff that the intercessors get through to him. In this respect they have privileges that only administrative and ministry elders share. He says, "I value both their prayer concern and the insights I receive from them."

Showdown at high noon. Pastor Walker and the church leader had scheduled a meeting, which was a close equivalent to what might be referred to as a showdown at high noon. The harmony of the church was at stake. However, before the meeting one of the intercessors called Paul Walker.

"God has been speaking to me, pastor," she said. "Do you have some important meeting coming up soon?" She, of course, had no information in the natural about what was going on in the high levels of the church administration, but God had told her in the Spirit about the meeting.

When Paul Walker affirmed that such a meeting was indeed coming up, she told him that she thought God was telling her what he should say in the meeting and what Scripture he was to use. God at the moment gave him a deep sense of agreement and confirmation. He obeyed and it worked beautifully!

The meeting was peaceful and harmonious. The church leader and those under his influence received the expanded vision and a new dimension of church outreach was achieved. Mount Paran has now been using the church campus for years and since that time has added a third campus and a fourth is in the works at the time of this writing.

Paul and I discussed the fact that many churches split because senior pastors are not sensitive to God's revelation through spiritually mature persons in the congregation. Some would have said, "Why would God give information like this to a little old grandmother in tennis shoes who lives in a two-bit apartment? Why wouldn't God give the information directly to me? *I'm* the spiritual leader of this church. *I'm* the one who hears from God about where our church is going. Who does she think she is to tell me how to run my church?"

Unfortunately, this attitude is widespread. But I believe God is raising up high-profile leaders such as Paul Walker to be role models for the rest of us—leaders who have no apologies to make about their maturity, their educational attainments, their spiritual depth and discernment, their leadership skills, the growth of their churches or the spiritual levels of their congregations.

These high-profile leaders have gained prominence, but they are also humble enough to know they are not spiritually self-sufficient. They understand the power of intercession as well as Joshua did in the battle of Rephidim. Whether their intercessors have the stature of a Moses or whether they are grandmothers in tennis shoes, they are ready to hear the voice

---

Humility is the opposite of arrogance, but there is some danger that undue humility can get in the way of receiving intercession.

---

of God and receive the additional spiritual power they need through these precious individuals.

How Moody learned the lesson. Through intercessors, Dwight L. Moody narrowly avoided the trap of spiritual arrogance and blossomed into the influential giant of the faith as we now know him. Moody was already a popular preacher. Even Abraham Lincoln had made a point of visiting Moody's Sunday School in Chicago. But something was lacking, namely a yielding to the full power of the Holy Spirit. I am indebted to Mark Bubeck who tells the story of how it happened, in his excellent book *Overcoming the Adversary.*[8]

After one of Moody's meetings two ladies approached him and said, "Mr. Moody, we have been praying for you." Reflecting some apparent spiritual arrogance, Moody replied rather abruptly, "Why don't you pray for the people?"

The ladies said quietly, "Because you need the power of the Holy Spirit."

Somewhat taken aback, Moody could only respond, "*I* need the power?" The thought was rather preposterous to a spiritual leader who had been visited by the President of the United States.

But the women had heard the Lord well. They customarily sat in the front row of his meetings, deep in prayer as he preached. At first he was annoyed, but gradually God softened his heart and he began to encourage not only their prayers, but the formation of prayer groups to beseech God that he would be endued with power. Then one day in New York City, Moody had such an experience of the filling with the Holy Spirit that he admitted he was never able to describe it in words.

One of his biographers says, "God seems to have answered in a mighty way the prayers of these two women, for at this time his life changed considerably from that of a young, somewhat cocky and proud preacher, to a humble, soft and mellow-hearted preacher."

When Moody's spiritual arrogance diminished, the power of God through faithful intercessors was released in his life and ministry.

5. Undue Humility

Humility is the opposite of arrogance, but there is some danger that undue humility can get in the way of receiving intercession. I have had some problems with this myself.

The thinking goes like this: *I am no better than anyone else in the Body of Christ. We are all sinners saved by grace. God loves all of His children equally. He does not love me more than the others. Why, then, should I expect to receive this powerful intercession when many of my church members do not have the same privilege? Instead of building a special team of prayer partners for myself, might it not be better just to encourage all church members to pray for each other?*

This is not biblical humility, because it fails to recognize that pastors and other leaders are, because of their office, not equal to every other member of the Body of Christ. I explained this

"Not to think of oneself highter than we ought to think."

matter in great detail in chapter 3, "Why Pastors Need Intercession," so there is no need to repeat it here. Pastors need intercessory prayer more than any other member of the congregation, and God's plan is to provide it for them.

The part I struggled with was a subsequent question: Why should I ask someone to give me 1 hour a day in prayer, when I give them back maybe 10 seconds a day? It doesn't seem fair.

I am now comfortable with the fact that this is also God's design. My intercessors pray for me much more than I pray for them, and they expect nothing different. God does things through me and my spiritual gifts that He is not doing through my intercessors. And He does things through them that He does not do through me.

In conclusion, I feel that a full appreciation of the operation of the Body of Christ is a vital key to ridding ourselves of the obstacles that are in the way of receiving personal intercession.

Intercessors may often not be very visible, but they are like the glands in our body that, 24 hours a day, secrete the hormones we need for life, health and energy. Once we understand this, ignorance, rugged individualism, fear, spiritual arrogance and undue humility will maintain no further foothold in our beings. We will be open to the full ministry of the Holy Spirit and His gifts through the Body of Christ to be all God wants us to be.

▬ REFLECTION QUESTIONS ▬

1. Discuss the difference between *saying* the Lord's Prayer and *praying* the Lord's Prayer. What are the six evident divisions of the Lord's Prayer, and what would each one include?
2. The phrase, "I'll be praying for you" can mean much or it can mean very little. What are some concrete examples of each?

3. Do you think this chapter is too critical of Jimmy Swaggart? Talk about how the issues raised relate to his personal problems.
4. Review the story of Paul Walker and his willingness to receive input from his intercessors. Why do you think many other pastors could not do this?
5. If a Christian leader resists receiving intercession for one or more of the reasons given, what can be done to change this?

Notes
1. Charles Henry Robinson, *The Conversion of Europe* (London, England: Longmans, Green and Co., 1917), p. 378.
2. Colin Whittaker, *Seven Guides to Effective Prayer* (Minneapolis, MN: Bethany House Publishers, 1987), p. 111.
3. Richard J. Foster, "The PTL Scandal," *Charisma & Christian Life*, March 1988, pp. 39-44.
4. Gordon MacDonald, *Rebuilding Your Broken World* (Nashville, TN: Oliver Nelson, 1988), p. 200.
5. Jimmy Swaggart, "From Me to You," *The Evangelist*, April 1987, p. 58.
6. Jimmy Swaggart, "The Lord of Breaking Through," *The Evangelist*, March 1988, p. 7.
7. "Swaggart's Confession," *Charisma & Christian Life*, April 1988, p. 20.
8. Mark I. Bubeck, *Overcoming the Adversary* (Chicago, IL: Moody Press, 1984), pp. 44,45.

Three Types of Personal Intercessors

PASTORS AND OTHER CHRISTIAN LEADERS WHO ARE OPEN to receive personal intercession and who ask God for it should soon find that intercession makes a measurable difference in their ministries. I fully recognize there are also many benefits of intercession that defy measurement, and sometimes they can be the most important. But the tangible benefits will also raise both our faith and our spirits.

God provides intercession in a variety of forms. Most of this chapter will deal with three kinds of personal intercessors committed to pray on a regular basis for a certain pastor, but we need to recognize that God moves in other ways as well.

D. L. MOODY'S INVALID INTERCESSOR

In the previous chapter, we were introduced to the two intercessors God used to open Dwight L. Moody to personal intercession. He was later involved in a dramatic incident that shows how God can touch an intercessor specifically for one event. At times God will assign what I have called a crisis intercessor to a particular task, rather than a personal intercessor.

This incident happened when Moody visited England in 1872 on a kind of sabbatical while his new church was being built in Chicago. His main purpose was to listen to and learn from some of England's great preachers. But one Sunday he broke his routine and agreed to minister in a church in London.

The Sunday morning turned out to be a disastrous experience. He confessed afterward that he never had such a hard time preaching in his life. Everything was perfectly dead. Then the horrible thought came to him that he had to preach there again that night. He only went through with it because he had given his word he would do so.

But what a difference! That evening the church was packed and there was a new and vital spiritual atmosphere. Moody said, "The powers of an unseen world seemed to have fallen upon the audience." Although he had not premeditated it, he decided to give an invitation for people to accept Jesus Christ as their personal Savior and was astounded when 500 people stood up. He repeated the invitation twice more to attempt to filter out the insincere, but all 500 went to the vestry to pray to receive Christ. A major revival started in that church and neighborhood that night!

And the intercession?

A woman who had attended the morning service returned home and told her invalid sister that a certain Mr. Moody from Chicago had preached. The invalid sister turned pale. "Mr. Moody from Chicago?" she asked in astonishment. "I read about him some time ago in an American paper and I have been praying to God to send him to London and to our church. If I had known he was going to preach this morning, I would have eaten no breakfast and spent the whole time he was preaching in prayer for him. Now, sister, go out of the room, lock the door, send me no dinner; no matter who comes don't let them see me. I am going to spend the whole afternoon and evening in prayer!"

This story is told by E. M. Bounds, who comments, "So while Mr. Moody stood in the pulpit that had been like an ice-chamber in the morning, the bedridden saint was holding him up before God, and in the evening God, who ever delights to answer prayer, poured out His Spirit in mighty power."[1]

GARY GREENWALD'S TEAM

God frequently empowers ministry through a team of intercessors. Gary Greenwald, pastor of the Eagle's Nest church in Irvine, California, had been conducting annual evangelistic crusades in Hawaii. Attendance had grown to 2,000 after several years. As they prayed about it they decided to step out in faith one year and rent the Hilton Hawaiian ballroom, which seats 4,000. It cost thousands of dollars, and they would need large crowds to pay their bill.

They sent a team of intercessors from their church in Irvine to stay in the Hilton Hawaiian one week before the crusade for fasting and prayer. The spiritual warfare was intense that week. The leader of the team suffered so much anxiety during the nights that he almost capitulated and returned home. Several of the team were afflicted with sicknesses of one kind or another. But they persisted and felt they were winning the battle. A big question was: Would they ever fill the ballroom?

The first 3 nights of the crusade they drew 3,000 people. The final 2 nights saw the ballroom packed out at 4,000. It was one of the most powerful crusades they had ever conducted. Many conversions and healing miracles took place, such as a severed Achilles tendon being completely healed. The spiritual warfare had been done and the crusade itself was easy.

They rented the ballroom again the following year. But sending the intercessory team for that week had been very expensive so they decided not to do it again. Hawaii usually has an open atmosphere for preaching, but this year the crusade was a disaster! The highest attendance was only 1,800. Divisions occurred among the leadership. Serious problems occurred over the worship leaders. It was a financial wipeout.

Gary Greenwald learned about the value of teams of intercessors the hard way that year.

PERSONAL INTERCESSORS

God uses crisis intercessors as we saw with D. L. Moody and teams of intercessors as with Gary Greenwald. He also uses personal intercessors, those who make a commitment to pray over an extended period of time for a particular pastor or other Christian leader.

As I have studied the phenomenon of personal intercession for several years in the role of a participant observer, I have found it useful to separate personal intercessors into three approximate categories. I like to think of personal intercession as operating in three concentric circles around the leader. (See top of next page)

- The inner circle. Here we picture the pastor along with what I will call I-1 intercessors.
- The middle circle. This contains I-2 intercessors.
- The outer circle. This contains I-3 intercessors.

Think of the I-1 intercessors as having a *close* relationship to the pastor, the I-2 intercessors as having a *casual* relationship, and the I-3 intercessors as having a *remote* relationship to the pastor. I will describe them from the outside in.

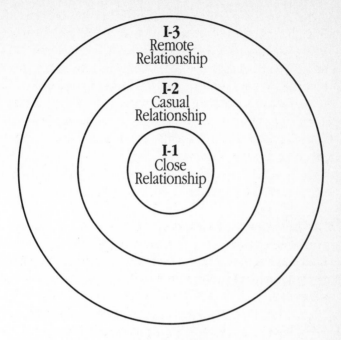

I-3 INTERCESSORS

I-3 intercessors can be quite remote from the pastor or leader they pray for. Most I-3 intercession is a one-way relationship. The leader often does not know who the I-3 intercessor is or that he or she is praying for them and their ministry. I think of Billy Graham, for example. Many intercessors have prayed faithfully for Billy Graham and his ministry for years without ever having so much as seen the evangelist in person. However, Billy Graham will be the first to tell you that such intercessors have made all the difference in the world in the effectiveness of his evangelistic ministry.

Of course, a certain amount of visibility beyond the local parish is needed in order to attract these kind of I-3 intercessors. Campus Crusade's Bill Bright says, "I would assume that there are hundreds, if not thousands, who pray for me daily from grade school through senior citizens." If it were not for such intercessors, Bright says, "I am sure I would have been dead long ago from physical exhaustion and would have been totally incapable of doing all that God has enabled me to do."

My friend Omar Cabrera, whose Vision of the Future Church of more than 100,000 in Argentina is one of the world's largest, has a unique system for recruiting I-3 intercessors. He simply asks his church members and families to pray for him and his wife, Marfa, when they say grace at meals. A recent calculation estimates that they probably receive 20,000 prayers a day through this appeal.

My wife, Doris, and I have a growing list of I-3 intercessors whose names and addresses we know at this moment. Some of them have international reputations such as Dick Eastman, Jack McAlister, Quin Sherrer, Jim Montgomery, Archie Parrish, Gary Bergel and others. Some of them we know only by name since we have never met them personally. Several are members of our 120 Fellowship Sunday School class. Others are old-time friends or former students. Many have the spiritual gift of intercession. Some pray primarily for us. Others have a long list of leaders they also pray for such as Jack McAlister who prays daily for more than 200 leaders and others. And I am sure we have I-3 intercessors whose names are not on the list.

A memorable experience occurred one day when I was standing in the crowded lobby of the Osaka Hilton Hotel in Japan. A perfect stranger, a Caucasian, walked up to me and said, "Are you Peter Wagner?" When I told him I was, he shared that he had prayed for me every morning for the past six years, and was pleased to finally meet me in person. I thanked him, took his name, and wrote him a letter, but I never received a reply. I have no idea where he came from or where he went. He seems like a modern Melchizedek!

My favorite I-3 intercessor is two-and-a-half-year-old Jess

Rainer. His father, Southern Baptist Pastor Thom Rainer, was doing a Ph.D. at Southern Baptist Theological Seminary and writing his dissertation on Peter Wagner. Needless to say, we kept in close touch during the process. In the midst of it, he wrote me a letter and discussed an academic matter or two. Then he added a paragraph that said, "By the way, my youngest son (two-and-a-half-year-old Jess) has heard your name so much that he concludes all of his prayers as follows: '...and thank you God for Peter Wagner, in Jesus' name, Amen'" May Jess's numbers multiply!

I-2 INTERCESSORS

Typical I-2 intercessors will have a regular, but somewhat casual, contact with the pastor or leader they pray for. Pastors' I-2 intercessors will see them in the pulpit every Sunday and shake hands when they go out the church door after the service. They may cross paths from time to time in other church-related events. But for many, this is about the extent of the personal contact.

One of the things I am suggesting in this book is that pastors take steps to cultivate contacts with I-2 intercessors. Most pastors I know experience from time to time a certain person in the line of those leaving the church service gives them an especially warm handshake and says, "Pastor, I pray for you every day!" We often take that as a formality and do not pay any more attention to it than we do to the statement, "I enjoyed the sermon." But in many cases there might be more to it than simply a formality. At least it is a pathway worth following because it might lead to discovering a personal intercessor truly anointed by God for supporting us in prayer.

A well-developed team of I-2 intercessors enjoys a two-way contact with the pastor. It is therefore essential to know who the I-2 intercessors are. Later on I will discuss the ways and means of identifying, screening, recruiting, servicing and maintaining these prayer partners. They obviously need to be kept better informed than I-3 intercessors. They also need to make themselves available to be called on for special prayer if and when a necessity arises.

The optimum size of a group of I-2 intercessors is not yet known, mainly because we do not have a large enough number of viable examples to work with. John Maxwell likes his group

---

It is clear in Matthew 25 that God is the One who decides who gets what talents and how many.

---

to be 100, although not more. He has a waiting list of those who would like to be enrolled as prayer partners and he lets new ones in only as openings occur. I do think there is an upward limit of I-2 intercessors, but this would not apply to I-3s.

The main principle as I see it is to maintain a reasonably high level of commitment among I-2 intercessors, and that comes through a certain amount of intentional personal contact as I will detail later on. Therefore, the number of I-2 intercessors should not become too large to sustain necessary contact. It will take time. Some time on our schedules needs to be set aside for this contact. How much time is reasonable and appropriate is a question that must be answered in each individual case.

My wife, Doris, and I have 18 I-2 intercessors on our prayer team. Ten of them are members of our 120 Fellowship Sunday School class: Sandra Gilbreath, George and Pam Marhad, Joanna McClure, Dave and Jane Rumph, Erick and Joanna Stone, Lil Walker and Mary Wernle. Two, David and Maureen Anderson, attend another church in the area. Four are from Texas: Elizabeth Alves, Cindy Jacobs, Bobbye Byerly and Jane Anne Pratt. One, Mary Lance Sisk, lives in North Carolina, and one, Jean Steffenson, lives in Colorado.

Somewhat predictably, 14 of the 18 are women. There again is the approximately 80 percent I mentioned earlier.

The Gift of Intercession

Not all of our intercessors have the gift of intercession, although I think God has chosen to allow us the privilege of a rather high percentage of those with the gift for reasons I will mention later. Of our 18 I-2 intercessors, 10 (Elizabeth Alves, Maureen Anderson, Bobbye Byerly, Cindy Jacobs, Joanna McClure, Jane Anne Pratt, Mary Lance Sisk, Jean Steffenson, Mary Wernle and Lil Walker) have been recognized as having a gift of intercession.

Doris and I consider the eight who do not have the gift of intercession as essential and precious to ourselves and our ministry as those who do. Some who do not have the gift are actually more committed to supporting us day in and day out than some who do. The center and guards are no less important on a football team than the running backs and the ends. It takes the whole group as a team to win.

Because this kind of language is relatively new to our Christian community in general, the process of absorbing its implications takes time. Pam Marhad is a key member of our team. But she had to work through her role as an I-2 intercessor as one who does not have a spiritual gift of intercession. She wrote about her experience in *Body Life*, our Sunday School class monthly newsletter. She said, "More often than not, when I decide I will pray for certain people or situations, a feeling of frustration and 'what's the use?' overcomes my good intentions and defeats me."

As she prayed about it, Pam felt the Lord took her to the parable of the talents in Matthew 25. There it is clear that God is the One who decides who gets what talents and how many.

When she saw that, she confessed, "I've been guilty of looking around and saying in my heart, 'Lord, I'm just a one-talent pray-er.' Others You have made five-talent pray-ers—let them pray. My prayers probably don't matter."

Then Pam rightly concludes that all God expects of her is to use the resources He has given her, nothing more, nothing less. "As I'm faithful and obedient to use what He's given," Pam says, "then He's free to give me more if He chooses. If I don't value His gifts to me and neglect them because they don't measure up to what I see others doing, then I very effectively tie the Lord's hands in my life and find myself on the outside looking in with envy and resentment."[2] It could not be said better.

When we invite I-2 intercessors to be part of the prayer partners team, we expect that the relationship will continue for an indefinite period of time. However, we recognize that God will assign us intercessors for a season, then give them other assignments, and we are open to that as well. Since we first formed our team of prayer partners in 1988, several have dropped off and several have been added. We expect this to continue, although we relate to all of them at any time as if our relationship will continue for many years.

Doris and I are the only leaders for whom some of our I-2 intercessors have committed themselves to pray regularly, but others pray on the same level for several leaders. Bobbye Byerly, for example, who is one of the national and international leaders of Women's Aglow Fellowship, is also committed as a personal intercessor for Jane Hansen, Joy Dawson, Cindy Jacobs and Mary Lance Sisk. Part of Bobbye's highly developed ministry of personal intercession is a keen sensitivity to the dancing Spirit of God over the people she prays for. For a season she will find God burdening her more for one than the others, then it might change.

As I write this (possibly *because* I am writing this book), a note just received from Bobbye Byerly says, "Peter, you are coming up No. 1 in my prayer discharge right now. It's nothing I've done or failed to do. Nothing you've done. I would guess that God is orchestrating a new realm of prayer support for you at this time."

Feeling the Wind of the Spirit

A few months ago, Doris and I were making a trip to England to do a pastors' seminar. Just before we left, one of our prayer partners, Dave Rumph, who is a research engineer at our local Xerox branch, said he sensed that the Lord was arranging something special in England with Roger Forster, whom I had never met personally. My assigned ministry in England had nothing directly to do with Roger or the Ichthus movement he leads.

Bobbye Byerly also phoned with a prophetic word she had received, and which I asked her to write out for me. In part it said, "Feel the wind of My Spirit. I am lifting you higher and higher. You need no effort on your part for My wind will lift you. Greater days are ahead. Far more than you can yet see are My plans for you."

Sure enough, the trip to England became a milestone in our ministry. Not so much because of my scheduled pastors' seminar, but because of an unplanned meeting with Roger Forster and Gerald Coates, two of the leaders of the March for Jesus movement. In that meeting, God began to give direction to Doris and me to take leadership of what we now call "A Day to Change the World" on June 25, 1994, in connection with the United Prayer Track of the A.D. 2000 Movement, which we also coordinate. The plans developing for this are "far more than we could see" before we went to England. It could turn out to be the largest prayer meeting in Christian history.

Here were two I-2 intercessors who were so tuned in to our ministry and God's plans for us that God used them and their prayers (as well as the prayers of others) to move us into an incredibly exciting and potentially awesome new area of service for God's Kingdom.

I do most of my teaching at Fuller in one-week or two-week modules. When I do them in one week, I teach mornings and afternoons each day. It is a concentrated schedule, but teaching usually stimulates and increases my energy level rather than diminishing it. A couple of years ago, one of my one-week church growth classes was not going well. On the Saturday before I began feeling washed out. Sunday also. When I began teaching on Monday I had no energy and I felt as though I was carrying a heavy load on my shoulders. Tuesday was almost as bad. But on Wednesday the load lifted, I could relax while I taught, and I could think clearly and creatively for the first time since Saturday.

Soon afterward three of our I-2 intercessors, Mary Wernle, Cindy Jacobs and Joanna McClure, approached me one at a time and said, "What happened last Wednesday? Why did I feel you needed special prayer for that day?" When I told them, we rejoiced together that God had coupled us in ministry and that the answers to prayer were so tangible.

I-1 INTERCESSORS

God calls I-1 intercessors to have a special close relationship with the pastor or other leader. Sometimes this involves a close social relationship, sometimes it is a largely spiritual relationship. Most, if not all, of the I-1 intercessors I know have the spiritual gift of intercession. Through it they have developed an intimacy with the Father that allows them to hear the Father's voice and know His purposes more clearly than most.

The leaders I know who relate to I-1 prayer partners sometimes have three of them, sometimes two, but most frequently one. Through the years, God has assigned two of them to us. The first was Cathy Schaller who was assigned to us for seven years. The second is Alice Smith, our current I-1 intercessor. They are both extremely powerful women in spiritual things, and both of them were first bonded to us in prayer through extraordinary circumstances.

THE LADDER AND THE FALL

The memorable day of our bonding with Cathy Schaller was March 25, 1983. I went out to our garage at 8:30 that evening to get some income tax papers. I had stored them up on a loft in the garage, which was 10 feet off the cement floor. As I had been doing for years, I climbed the stepladder to get onto the loft. My head was 12 feet above the floor when I began moving from the ladder to the loft.

Then in an instant something pulled that ladder out from under me (I have chosen those words carefully!) and I took a free fall, landing on the back of my head, my neck and my upper back. During the second or so it took to complete the fall, I was thinking to myself, "This is it!" but I also was able to shout loudly enough so that Doris came running to the garage. My next-door neighbor, Randy Becker, heard the commotion and rushed over. He and Doris called the paramedics and prayed.

The ambulance came and took me to the emergency room at St. Luke's Hospital. They put me through all the tests and X rays and a couple of hours later sent me home. Remarkably, they found no structural damage or internal injuries. I was badly bruised, stiff and sore for about six weeks, but had no after effects at all from what was the most serious accident of my life.

That evening Cathy Schaller and her husband, Mike, who is a school psychologist, had taken a group of young girls to a Ken Medema concert in a church about 10 miles from my home. Cathy at that time was in her late 20s, and was working part-time as a speech therapist. They had three children who were not with them that evening. Some months previously they had joined Lake Avenue Congregational Church and the 120 Fellowship, but we had not known each other well as yet.

A Life and Death Battle

When Mike and Cathy returned to their seats after an intermission, Cathy happened to notice that her watch said 8:30. They began to dim the house lights for effect when an incredibly powerful cloud of evil darkness seemed to envelop Cathy. The presence of evil was so strong around her that she could smell it. In her spirit she identified it as a spirit of death and destruction. The Holy Spirit said to her, "It has come to destroy someone you have a relationship to, but not one of your children." She felt a shield of protection raised between the force of evil and her own being, so she knew she was personally safe.

Without hesitation, Cathy began to pray under her breath for "legions of angels." Then a severe pain came into her back. It felt as though her back was breaking. She squirmed with pain and Mike whispered, "What's wrong?" All she could say was, "My spirit is troubled and my back hurts." Mike laid on hands and prayed that her back would be healed. Cathy continued to pray in the Spirit under her breath for 20 minutes, then sensed a total release. The battle was over, the evil cloud left, she relaxed, enjoyed the rest of the concert and went home to bed.

Late that night her bedside telephone rang. It was our Sunday School class president alerting the class prayer chain to pray for me because I had suffered a terrible accident. Cathy instantly knew in her spirit what she had prayed for at the concert, but the president could not confirm the exact time of the fall.

The next morning Cathy's call to Doris and me was one of the most incredible telephone calls I can remember. We could not prove it in a court of law, but Doris and I do not need a court of law to be convinced that Cathy's faithfulness in prayer that night literally saved my physical life. Satan had sent an evil spirit (which we later located, but that is another story) to kill me. For years and years after that, Doris and I took Cathy and Mike out to dinner every March 25 to celebrate my deliverance from "The Fall" and express our gratitude to her for ministering to us.

Seven Years of Learning

"The Fall" incident was the dramatic beginning of a prayer partner relationship of seven years, which ultimately changed the

> We learned that the top intercessors need intercessory help themselves during critical times.

P. 134

direction of our lives and ministry. At the beginning none of us knew much about prayer or personal intercession.

Cathy recalls that some time before the incident someone casually mentioned to her that she might have the gift of intercession. Subsequently she received internal impressions about relatives who were in danger on two separate occasions, but had no idea how to respond to them. Both of them died! You can imagine how grateful I am that the third time she did respond. When she called me the next morning, I said, "Cathy, do you know that this is a gift of intercession?"

Through the years, Cathy related to Doris and me as our first I-1 intercessor. Those were the years the seed thoughts for the content of this entire book were planted. She was learning what it meant to be an intercessor. We were learning how to receive intercession. We had our ups and our downs, and we needed both of them to learn what we know now.

After seven years, Cathy's gift had developed to the extent that God released her from her assignment to the Wagners and assigned her to be the full-time prayer leader for DAWN

Ministries, an international mission agency promoting saturation church planting. She is now an ordained minister and an intercessor for James Montgomery, DAWN's president, and his wife, Lyn.

Few people have had the profound effect on our lives, careers and ministries as has Cathy Schaller. Her name will come up on several other occasions as the book moves on.

INTERCESSORS NEED HELP TOO

One of the things we learned about I-1 intercessors is that they, particularly during critical times, need intercessory help themselves. The spiritual warfare they find themselves engaged in on behalf of the pastor or leader can become overwhelming. Moses, for example, would not have been able to intercede effectively for Joshua without the timely help of Aaron and Hur as he fought the battle of Rephidim. I recall one time when Cathy desperately needed her Aarons and Hurs.

During the 1980s, I had invited John Wimber to help me teach a new course on Signs, Wonders and Church Growth at Fuller Seminary. It eventually stirred up a very intense controversy and I was in the center of it for years. This was by far the most painful experience I have personally had since leaving the mission field in Bolivia. And it lasted for three and a half years!

Without going into details here, by the end of three and a half years I had come to the end of my patience. I had been on the defensive for all that time and I was prepared to switch to the offensive. A crucial meeting had been scheduled with the seminary Faculty Senate. My temper was on edge and my guns were loaded for the showdown. I went to the meeting. A grim-faced dean entered and put my book *How to Have a Healing Ministry* on the table in front of him. A distinguished theological professor did the same. I knew very well that both of them had higher IQs than I did. I thought I was in for it!

But the meeting was called to order and there was no show-down. The proposal I presented was passed unanimously. No one was nasty. A couple of rather routine questions were addressed to me, nothing else. I had my guns loaded, but did not have to pull the trigger. Why? The spiritual warfare behind the whole scenario had been done before the meeting began. I believe that Cathy as my I-1 intercessor was the principal agent for winning that spiritual battle.

But it was not easy for her by any means. Looking back, I am convinced that this Faculty Senate meeting was a significant milestone in my personal ministry career, if not also for Fuller Seminary. Because of that, the warfare was more intense than usual.

During the days leading up to that meeting, Cathy experienced several devastating events.

- Cathy's car was totalled and she received a serious whiplash. The other driver was clearly at fault, but they were suing Cathy!
- The family of a student in the Christian junior high school where Cathy was then teaching had pressed a written list of 30 trumped-up charges against her competence and character. She was emotionally devastated. The charges were being taken to her school board, which coincidentally was meeting to consider them on the same day our Faculty Senate was meeting.
- Cathy's kitchen caught on fire, and the fire burned a hole through her kitchen floor.

Aarons and Hurs
More than ever before, Cathy needed her Aarons and Hurs. And God sent them.

The first one we knew about was Dave Rumph, an I-2 intercessor who does not have the gift of intercession, but does have a recognized gift of encouragement. God assigned Dave to pray for Cathy at that time, but especially to call her on the telephone several times the preceding week to encourage her.

After the fact, we learned about eight others who had prayer for Cathy. Christy Graham, whom I have previously mentioned as an example of a crisis intercessor, had been assigned by God to pray intensely for Cathy six weeks before the Faculty Senate meeting, and she had been praying faithfully every day.

Lil Walker, who is now one of our I-2 intercessors but at that time was not, was assigned to pray for Cathy. Linda Stanberry, a furloughed missionary taking my courses at Fuller, received a week-long burden to pray for Cathy. Nanette Brown, a member of our Sunday School class, was awakened by God at 3:30 A.M. the morning of Cathy's school board meeting and she prayed for Cathy for three-quarters of an hour before going back to sleep. The other four were Yvonne Lindsey, Joanna McClure and Elizabeth Philip from our Sunday School class, and one of the teachers in Cathy's school.

Cathy was doing what Euodia and Syntyche did for the apostle Paul: spiritual warfare on my behalf. I did not have to go through the potentially explosive Faculty Senate debate I had anticipated. Cathy took the brunt of the spiritual attack for me. It never occurred to her to complain. She was using her spiritual gift and flowing with the Holy Spirit, and her prayers for me were being answered. But she needed help. None of the nine people who helped her was praying for me at the time. Satan was trying to get Cathy's arms down (to use the analogy of Moses praying for Joshua), but God provided her the nine Aarons and Hurs.

The results of their prayers? The lawsuit from the accident was dropped; the school board dismissed the charges totally; the fire insurance paid for rebuilding Cathy's kitchen floor much better than it had been before the fire. She told us that the week after the Faculty Senate meeting was one of the most relaxed, pleasant and less stressful weeks she could remember both in her school and with her family. The battle had been fought and won!

A helpful analysis of what happens spiritually in situations like this comes from Sylvia R. Evans of Elim Bible Fellowship in Lima, New York. She says that one of God's most wonderful blessings is His faithfulness "to waken intercessors for the 'night watch' or an 'early morning watch' and to place them on duty to hold off the enemy." She sees intercessors as watchmen constantly on the alert to be assigned their position in battle.

Speaking of the full armor of God in Ephesians 6, Evans interprets the passage as suggesting that the intercessor "is to be able to aggressively withstand the enemy, taking the attack for others who may be the real target. The watchman must be able to quench all the fiery darts, not only against himself or herself, but also against the ones for whom they are standing watch."[3]

Doris and I are thankful to God for raising up intercessors willing and able to take the fiery darts of the enemy for us. They are the most precious group of people related to our lives and our ministry. And we rejoice as we see God spreading this kind of spiritual power more and more widely throughout the Body of Christ these days.

■ REFLECTION QUESTIONS ■

1. This chapter gives illustrations of how prayer affected the ministries of D.L. Moody and Gary Greenwald. Could you give an example of how a similar thing happened for a leader you know?

2. Mention some people you know who serve as I-3 intercessors for pastors or other leaders, and talk about that relationship.

3. Pam Marhad's experience is helpful to many Christians who desire to serve God with all their hearts. Why is it that so many can identify with her?
4. What do you think actually happened in the heavenlies when Cathy Schaller prayed for Peter Wagner during his fall from the ladder?
5. As this chapter shows, serious intercession for a pastor or other leader can open one to severe attacks of the enemy. Some question whether it is worth the risk. What do you think?

Notes
1. E. M. Bounds, *The Complete Works of E. M. Bounds on Prayer* (Grand Rapids, MI: Baker Book House, 1990), pp. 360,361.
2. Pam Marhad, "Using Our Gifts to God's Glory," *Body Life*, February 1990, p. 7.
3. Sylvia R. Evans, "Watching in Prayer," *Intercessors for America Newsletter*, June 1989, p. 2.

Recruiting Prayer Partners

THIS MAY BE THE MOST VITAL CHAPTER OF THE BOOK FOR many pastors and other Christian leaders who desire to see the power of personal intercession begin to flow through their lives and ministries. Satan is not ignorant of the threat that intercession for pastors poses to his evil plans. He wants to mess up pastors and neutralize their spiritual influence in their churches and their communities to the highest degree possible. Intercessors, particularly the kind I have been describing, set back the enemy's work in a definite way wherever they go into action.

A well-known tactic the devil has all-too-skillfully employed in the past is to manipulate pastors into making poor choices of prayer partners. This can and does short-circuit receiving personal intercession in two ways.

The first way the enemy uses to discourage intercession is to cause pastors to choose wrong intercessors who end up doing them more harm than good. This is bad enough in itself, but it also leads to the second tactic. One bad experience can cause a pastor not only to give up on the concept altogether, but even to move from there and teach others that it is unwise. One prominent leader I know rejected personal intercession for himself for years. He taught many of his followers to reject it until recently God brought him into a close relationship with an intercessor who had high integrity and who caused him to change his mind.

RESULTS OF A POOR CHOICE

Because I teach personal intercession in my Doctor of Ministry seminars, many of my students become motivated to seek personal intercession. When they return to their churches they have functioning teams of prayer partners within weeks, at times even within days, where God had obviously already been preparing the way for them. The overwhelming majority of reports I get back are positive and enthusiastic. But not all. One of the pastors, who has an especially analytical mind, not only had a bad experience, but he turned it into a term paper for my advanced seminar.

This pastor from the Midwest writes under the pen name of Paul A. Freedman. He has enough personal stability and a high enough level of self-esteem not to be devastated by his negative experience. He thinks positively, learns from his setbacks, and moves forward aggressively on the basis of what he learns. No wonder his church is a growing church. He did and still does believe "intercessory prayer is one of the most important elements of successful ministry today." He said that since he first heard about personal prayer partners in my seminar, "I have come to greatly appreciate and rely upon the ministry of I-1 intercessors."

Paul Freedman's story illustrates what can happen when the

wrong people get into the crucial position of an I-1 intercessor, and then what can happen when the right people are there.

Paul had begun to look for an I-1 intercessor, and his church had another crucial need at the time. He had given high priority to leading a strong prayer ministry in his church, but as the church continued to grow he found he could give less and less

Intercessory prayer is one of the most important elements of successful ministry today.

time to it. This caused great frustration. It was obvious that the entire prayer ministry needed to be updated and reorganized.

Freedman says that he was happy and relieved when "a dearly loved and well-respected member of the church approached me to tell me that she had been praying specifically for me on a daily basis, and that she saw a great need to reorganize the prayer ministry of our church." So Paul saw this as meeting both needs. He invited her to become an I-1 intercessor for him and also to take charge of the church's prayer ministry.

From Doubts to Depression
Bad move! He says, "I was expecting relief and new strength, but things just got worse!"

She was an I-1 intercessor, so Paul began to share some of his more personal prayer requests with her. He soon noticed that she seemed to differ with him on certain theological points, but he regarded them as minor issues. He later found out that they had been major concerns for this woman.

As the arrangement continued, Freedman began to notice

his ministry seemed to be less effective. More people than usual were dissatisfied. He needed to put out higher levels of physical and mental energy to get the same results. He was always tired. He became angry. The anger led to frustration and the frustration led to depression. He says, "I was losing my love for the ministry. I knew the Lord was still there for me, but I didn't want to be there for the Lord anymore. I was angry with God and angry with myself. I just wanted out!"

Then the enemy, having Paul Freedman where he wanted him, unloaded the brunt of his attack. In one week, two women, unrelated to each other, came to him for "counseling." They had both developed an infatuation for him and they let him know that they would be available to him any time he had the desire. Fortunately, in Freedman's case, the internal alarm went off. He says, "I recognized the spiritual attacks for what they were. I quickly decided to get my wife and get away!"

They isolated themselves for a month, seeking new objectivity and a renewed relationship to God. The Lord met them in their need, and revealed to Paul Freedman what the core of the problem was. He saw clearly that the woman he had selected as an I-1 intercessor and asked to lead the church's prayer ministry was not God's choice. What he says is extremely important: "She was not submitted to my ministry nor open to my spiritual authority. Rather, she wanted to change me through prayer. She sought control of me by asking God to change me into something that she believed was correct."

The woman's negative influence meanwhile had spread. She turned some of the I-2 intercessors against the pastor and caused discontent, disunity, anger and even rebellion among church members. Several families left the church as a result.

Once he realized all of this, Pastor Freedman then faced what he thought would be his biggest headache of all. How would he tell this woman what he now knew without causing an explosion and a possible church split? She wielded a tremendous amount of influence in the congregation.

But God knew all about it and had gone ahead of Paul. Before the Freedmans returned from their vacation, the woman and her family had left the church, citing theological differences as the reason.

Replacing the False Intercessor

As it turned out, this incredibly smooth solution to a potential disaster happened because of positive intercessory prayer. Before Freedman returned from his vacation, God had replaced the former woman intercessor with what eventually became three new I-1 intercessors. None knew of the other two. All had been praying, and they had also been keeping journals of what the Lord was revealing to them for Paul. Each of them had been praying for him for months previously. Undoubtedly, it was the foothold of the enemy through the false intercessor that had prevented the pastor from recognizing them as intercessors sooner.

When the new intercessors compared notes, the consistency and agreement in what God was showing all three was overwhelming. Remarkably, two of the three had clearly known months previously that Paul would be tempted by "lustful and foolish" women. He rightly concludes, "The intercessors having received advanced warnings to pray for me at that time may well have saved my ministry."

And the upshot? In a few months a new prayer ministry was installed, and the church began to grow again. Paul Freedman says, "During a three-month period, under the prayers of God's chosen warriors, our church received into membership the largest number of new members in our history. We also witnessed average weekly offerings hit an all-time high."

The risk of making a mistake such as Freedman did comes with the territory. But I believe we can learn from him and

experiences of others and reduce such mistakes to a
n.

RECRUITING SHORT-TERM PRAY-ERS

None of what I have said so far should lead us to imagine that
the only prayer that pastors and other leaders need to receive
is that of recognized I-1, I-2 or I-3 intercessors. Many members
of my Sunday School class do not pray for me on a regular or
daily basis, for example, and yet they do pray through when
there is a special need. I consider it important to let them know
of my prayer requests in general, and some more specifically.
I share requests every week.

Sandra Gilbreath, one of our I-2 intercessors, also heads the
prayer ministry of the 120 Fellowship. Sandra gives leadership
to the prayer ministry in class time; she identifies and recruits
those who have a special desire to pray for people and needs
of the class; she leads a pre-class prayer meeting; she process-
es prayer request slips filled out in class; she organizes prayer
chains for special needs as required.

For example, when Doris or I or both of us go on some
ministry trips, Sandra organizes a prayer and fasting chain. We
do not request it on every trip and thereby we avoid it becoming a formality or a routine. But when we feel a certain ministry
will be a special target of spiritual warfare, Sandra organizes
her prayer chain.

Sandra typically will cut, paste and photocopy a page from
a date book that contains spaces for all the days we will be
gone, including one week after the trip. We have learned from
hard experience that frequently the most severe spiritual attacks
will come right after, not during, a certain ministry assignment.
Sandra then makes an announcement in class and passes the
prepared sheet around. Class members, whether they are Wagner prayer partners or not, fill their names in on one or more

days on which they promise to fast at least one meal and pray for us and for the ministry. Sandra then gives us a photocopy of the filled-in calendar, and she reminds those who have signed up when their day comes around.

I do not always do so, but I saved my copy of the prayer schedule from a recent trip to Argentina and Brazil containing some notes I had made on it. Each day has at least two persons praying and as many as four. The most visible attacks this time were physical. There, of course, may have been others I did not even know about because of the prayer. I see in my notes that at one point I lost my voice, once I had a stuffed-up head, once I had a serious cough, and once I had an acute attack of diverticulitis. All of these were unusually short lived, and none became a barrier of any sort to my ministry on those days. I believe that the enemy again was frustrated through prayer.

RECRUITING I-3 INTERCESSORS

There is usually some overlap between what I have called short-term pray-ers and I-3 intercessors. Theoretically there is no upward limit to the number of I-3 intercessors needed to support a given ministry. The one limitation I am aware of is the ability to keep them informed. Later I want to discuss this in some detail, but here I will simply mention that one way to keep the I-3 intercessors informed is through a regular letter to them. Writing and mailing such letters is where the actual number of persons on the list can increase the demands for resources of time, energy and money.

Doris and I currently have 101 I-3 intercessors to whom we send a periodic letter. We would like more than 101 people praying for us, and we probably do have an unknown number of others who also pray for us regularly. We try to keep the I-3 list to as high a level of commitment and quality as we can. We do not add names easily or haphazardly. I could pass out cards for people to fill in during my seminars and probably develop a mailing list of 10,000 over a period of time. But the commitment level would drop dramatically. Many of these would regard our letter as a newsletter and many, as the seminar became more distant in time, would habitually discard the letter without reading it.

On the other hand, no prayer is wasted. I would rather have 100 pastors pray for me for a week or two after a seminar than not have them pray at all. So I keep asking people to pray for us. Pastors should also do this week after week from their pulpits. The more personal the requests the better—to a point. Leaders of ministries should include prayer requests in their newsletters. And many pray-ers will respond positively.

But those who do respond should not be confused with I-3 intercessors lest the category become meaningless. Some may well turn out to be I-3s, but true I-3 intercessors, no matter how remote they are from the pastor or leader, have sensed a call from God to pray for the pastor on a regular basis, even though it is not necessarily daily. They expect their commitment to continue for a considerable period of time.

RECRUITING I-2 INTERCESSORS

I like the formula Cindy Jacobs recommends for recruiting I-2 intercessors. She uses Luke 11:9 where it tells us to *ask* and it will be given, *seek* and we will find, *knock* and it will be opened to us. *Asking*, according to the Jacobs Formula, is praying for the Lord to touch the potential personal prayer partners and prepare them. *Seeking* is to sit down and make a list of all those who from general observation or past experience seem as though they might be praying for you or willing to pray for you. *Knocking* is then getting in contact with those on the list by letter or by telephone.

Cindy says that when she first heard about personal prayer

partners she and her family were going through hard times. Her husband was having unusual problems on the job, the children were under severe harassment, and it seemed they were only moving from crisis to crisis. One day she said, "Enough is enough! I have had it with this attack!" So she prayed that the Lord would send personal intercessors. Then she made a list and contacted them, stressing that the prayer requests were to be considered confidential. The letter she wrote, she says, "explained that we would be sharing intimate details that were to be revealed to no one other than our prayer partners."[1]

What were the results? The response was tremendously encouraging. Within a week all the immediate problems cleared up. Cindy says, "The prayer partners for Generals of Intercession are all top notch intercessors, and we are greatly touched by their labor of love on our behalf. Since they have been praying for us our ministry has exploded in growth."[2]

Asking God

Some leaders who understand personal intercession feel they should not actively recruit I-2 intercessors, but should stop at the first part of the Jacobs Formula and simply ask God for them. This is the policy of Pastor Paul Walker of Mount Paran Church of God in Atlanta. As I mentioned in a previous chapter, he knows of 50 I-2 intercessors in his congregation who pray for him. They are mostly mature women. Each one of them, so far as he can keep track, was directly and individually called of God to that important ministry. Paul Walker told me personally that he used to have an I-1 intercessor, and would welcome another, but he feels that God should take the initiative and again is waiting on Him.

One of the most dramatic answers to prayer I have heard concerning I-2 intercessors occurred in Kenya. One of my students, Francis Kamau, who is an Assemblies of God pastor, said that he had three I-1 intercessors, but never had thought much about I-2s. This was before he learned my terminology, but it fit exactly when he learned it.

One day all three I-1s came to Francis and said that God was telling them he needed some more prayer partners, and that God would give them to him. The four of them covenanted to pray for I-2 intercessors for a week. On Friday of that week, Pastor Kamau received no fewer than 22 telephone calls, all saying, "Pastor, God has told me to pray for you!" I joked and asked him if he would lease me some of those I-1 prayer partners!

Seeking and Knocking

The second part of the Jacobs Formula, "seek and knock," also works well. Jerry Johnson has been the executive pastor of my church, Lake Avenue Congregational Church, for two decades. He became motivated to recruit prayer partners in 1986 when he first visited Korea and spent some time with God on one of the prayer mountains there. Since then he has increased his own prayer time to one hour, and he began asking God for I-2 intercessors. He then made a list and wrote to 40 people challenging them to promise to pray for him at least one day a week, and to indicate which day or days they would be praying.

Of the 40 people on Jerry's list, 31 responded and several committed more than 1 day or every day to pray for him. Jerry later reported to me that the number has gone up to 53 prayer partners. He knows that on some days at least six or seven are praying for him. He has noticed, and the church members have noticed, the increase in power in his ministry since he first recruited prayer partners.

Doris and I have seen both parts of the Jacobs Formula work. We began by recruiting our initial I-2 prayer partners team. In 1988, Cathy Schaller had been our I-1 intercessor for five years, so in order to learn more about how personal intercession works, Doris and I took Cathy and her family to San Diego for a weekend to have some R&R and also to research the prayer dynamic in Skyline Wesleyan Church under the leadership of John Maxwell. By the time we came home, we were convinced that we needed to take some action.

Forming the Team

At that time Cathy was also the leader of the Sunday School class pastoral care team, and she knew more about more of the members of the class than anyone else. So I called her and said, "Cathy, would you please make a list of the class members who you know are already praying for us on a regular basis, and then approach them one by one to see if they will commit themselves to an I-2 relationship with us. Above all, when you ask them, do it in such a way that they will be able to say no very easily if they do not feel God is calling them to do it."

I felt this was the wisest procedure, because if I had approached them personally I suspected that some, just out of their love and respect for me, could not bring themselves to say no, even if they really felt like it. It worked well, and we brought together our initial team of 13 I-2 intercessors who, with Cathy, made a prayer partners team of 14.

I do not recall how many said no, but I did make a mental note that one of them was Lil Walker, a class member known to have the spiritual gift of intercession. Lil told Cathy, and then me personally, that although God did direct her to pray for me from time to time, He had assigned her as an I-1 intercessor to our pastor, Paul Cedar, and that she did not feel free to take on any other regular commitments.

To complete the story, since then Paul Cedar has left, Lil was released from the assignment, and she is now one of our I-2 intercessors. But my point is that it is very important to allow people the greatest freedom to turn down the invitation if it does not seem right at the time. I myself, incidentally, was one of those who turned down Jerry Johnson's initial invitation. The last thing either of us needs is an intercessor like Paul Freedman's.

The Rule: Slow and Cautious

Even when God initiates the process, Doris and I have been very slow and cautious about inviting additional I-2 intercessors. A turning point in our ministry came at the great Lausanne Congress on World Evangelization held in Manila in the summer of 1989.

At the Lausanne Congress we sensed that God was putting strategic-level spiritual warfare high on our ministry agenda for the 1990s. We did not at that time know of the far-reaching scope of this change, but God did, and He began to provide for us some world-class intercessors to add to our team of I-2s. Truly, the intensity of the personal spiritual warfare we are now engaged in has escalated considerably, and we frankly need more help than previously.

The first additional I-2 intercessor was Cindy Jacobs, whom I have mentioned several times. We became acquainted earlier in 1989 at a Prayer Summit in Washington, D.C., and Doris and I formed a close personal friendship with Cindy and Mike. We did several things together, but it still took Doris and me several months before we approached Cindy to join our ministry as a prayer partner. She had known by the Holy Spirit for some time that we would invite her, but she patiently waited.

Cindy then introduced us to the next I-2 intercessor, Bobbye Byerly. We had never heard of Bobbye Byerly until we met her in Manila where she was part of the 24-hour intercession team praying for the Lausanne Congress. Cindy privately told us that Bobbye had one of the highest international reputations as an intercessor that she was aware of. We liked Bobbye and her husband, Jim, very much, but never dreamed God would give us this woman Cindy had spoken so highly of as a prayer partner.

One day near the end of the Manila conference Bobbye called us aside and said she wanted to talk to us. She told us she had not slept the night before, not a totally unusual report from an intercessor. But then she added that the reason God had kept her awake the whole night was to give her the assignment to pray for us! She told us there were only two others God had assigned her to pray for at that time, Jane Hansen and Joy Dawson.

Coming from a woman who was so widely respected for her ability to hear from God, this was astounding to us. Nevertheless, we, as always, were cautious. And Bobbye was very sweet about it, never at all pushy, even though she already knew what the final outcome would be. Yet, it took us four months to be convinced that the door was truly open. I later told her that it was a special challenge to pray for seminary professors because they are overly cautious. Even then, we hedged a bit by asking Cindy if she would call Bobbye and tell her how we felt, giving her plenty of space to say no to our request. She, of course, said yes, and we have a wonderful relationship.

RECRUITING I-1 INTERCESSORS

If it takes more care to recruit I-2 intercessors than I-3s, the greatest care needs to be exercised with I-1 intercessors. In this category I agree with Paul Walker that God Himself must be the one who initiates the contact. I think that the only advisable procedure for us who are pastors and leaders is to go directly to God and *ask* Him for them, starting and stopping with point one of the Jacobs Formula.

I have already related the incredible story of how God used Satan's plot to kill me in my garage to bond us with Cathy Schaller as our first I-1 intercessor. An equally supernatural event brought us together with our current I-1 intercessor, Alice Smith.

Doris and I were in Seoul, Korea, in the summer of 1990,

participating in Paul Yonggi Cho's annual Church Growth International conference. I am on Cho's board and I teach in his conference almost every year. That year we made a mistake that we have not repeated, deciding to hold the plenary teaching session in the Yoido Full Gospel church sanctuary instead of in one of the smaller chapels. The sanctuary seats 25,000, and as only 3,000 were in attendance at the conference, the most prominent thing we saw from the platform was empty seats.

"She Is an Intercessor"

Cho himself did the first session of teaching at the conference, and he had his board sit on the platform behind him. I must admit as I sat in the back row of the board members' section, my mind was not totally on Cho's teaching, excellent as it was. I had heard the same teaching every year for any number of years.

In fact, I will go so far as to confess that I had a yellow pad in my hands, but instead of taking notes, I was catching up on some urgent correspondence. I naturally looked up and nodded my head from time to time, and once when I did this, my eyes focused on a person sitting so far away that I could only tell it was a woman, but could not see any features. When I looked at her, God spoke very clearly in my spirit saying, "She is an intercessor!" I thought it was very nice that we had at least one intercessor in the audience and went on writing letters.

But twice more exactly the same thing happened. It was remarkable enough for me to make a mental note, but I thought nothing more about it until the break. I had also spotted two of my Fuller students in the audience and as I had not yet greeted them, I went off the platform and made my way back to where they were standing. They happened to be standing right next to the man whom I had taken to be the husband of the intercessor. She herself was standing abut 30 feet away talking to someone else.

After conversing with my students, I met the man, who

introduced himself as Eddie Smith, a pastor on the staff of Calvary Baptist Church, Houston, Texas. Somewhat impishly, I decided I would test Eddie with a couple of rather loaded questions concerning intercession to see if this Southern Baptist knew much about it. He answered them perfectly! Then I went over to his wife.

She told me her name was Alice Smith. I immediately said, "You're an intercessor, aren't you?" She raised her eyebrows and said, "How did you know?"

"God told me while I was up on the platform," I replied.

Alice started sobbing! "I can't believe I'm talking to you," she blurted. "Six months ago God told me to start praying for you and I have been praying for you constantly ever since. I never imagined I would actually meet you in person!"

The conversation went on from there. Among other things, Alice told me what a blessing an article on intercession I had written for the Vineyard magazine, *Equipping the Saints*, had been to her senior pastor, Steve Meeks. Doris and I then arranged to spend several hours with Alice and Eddie before we left Korea. At one point I asked Doris, "Do you think Alice might be a candidate for a new prayer partner?"

"What are we waiting for?" Doris said, "We'd better invite her before we leave!"

This was a radical departure from our usual procedure. Alice had been a total stranger, and we had waited three months before inviting an internationally-known intercessor such as Bobbye Byerly. But we both had a strong witness in our spirits that Alice was to be a prayer partner. So we asked her, and she immediately accepted because she had known for six months that God had assigned the job to her.

At that point Alice became an I-2 prayer partner. But a month or two later, as I was praying in my private prayer time, the word of the Lord came to me so strongly that for the first or second time I can ever remember I "journaled" the word. The whole thing was about my future direction and Alice Smith.

Among other things, God told me that Alice would be my most powerful intercessor. I asked God how this could be since Cathy Schaller had been my most powerful intercessor for years. He did not answer at that time, but a few weeks afterward He showed us that He was giving Cathy another assignment with DAWN Ministries. Meanwhile I had spoken to Alice about switching from an I-2 to an I-1. I marvel at the goodness of God in providing us a new I-1 intercessor even before reassigning the one He had so graciously given us for seven years.

Life-Saving Intercession
A couple of months after this, God seemed to seal this new relationship with a second incident in which I believe my physical life was again saved. The first one, where Cathy prayed for me as I fell off the ladder, involved several physical and tangible details, which indicated probable cause and effect, although, as I said, I could not prove in a court of law that her prayer saved my life. This second incident can only be interpreted in the Spirit and what might have happened to me had it not been for Alice's intercession is left to speculation.

Alice Smith, 40, is a mother of four and a real estate agent. She is a Bible teacher and conference speaker. She called me on November 23, 1990, to tell me what had happened to her on November 15. That day she had already been praying for Doris and me for two and a half hours, when a change came over her and an incredibly intense spiritual battle began. In more than 16 years of experience in high-level spiritual warfare, it was the most awesome attack she had been involved in. She logged 1:15 P.M. in her journal, and knew that I was in grave physical danger.

As she started to intercede, the Lord gave her a vision of a principality coming out of the south. Later information has led us to suspect that the source of this attack was the spirit of death, known as San La Muerte, which we had been battling in Argentina throughout most of 1990. The story of that front-line warfare in Argentina is told in my book, *Warfare Prayer* (Regal Books). Whether that spirit of death itself was directly involved or whether assignments had been passed through some sort of hierarchy of dark angels, we do not know.

Alice says, "The principality was as large as a man and it was hovering over Peter's left shoulder with an arrow in its

---

Filter out the flakes. Intercessors can and do appear on the scene for wrong motives.

---

hand pointing toward his heart. I was crying out, 'Save him, Lord! Have mercy and save him!' The Lord revealed that this was a spirit of death. I asked the Holy Spirit if Peter was okay, and He replied, 'His life is in the balance!' Travail then poured out of me! I was under such labor of prayer that I crawled to the phone and asked Eddie to pray. Eddie later told me he thought I was dying and he enlisted Pastor Steve Meeks and some of our other intercessors to help. The battle became more intense. I cried for mercy, reminding the Father of His plans for Peter, speaking the Scripture, warring the forces of darkness. Then at 1:57 P.M., as quickly as it began, it ended. I saw a warring angel of the Lord come and snatch the arrow from the principality's hand, break it in two over his knee, and leave westward! The spirit of death just disappeared."

Alice was totally fatigued. Her strength was gone. Her legs felt like spaghetti. She lay on the floor for an hour and a half after it was over before she could get up and go about her business.

And me? It would have occurred between 11 A.M. and 12 noon in my time zone on that day. Neither Doris nor I could recall any signs of danger around us at that time. Apparently, Alice had fended off the spirit of death much as a Patriot missile intercepted Scud missiles in the Persian Gulf War before they could land and explode. The apostle Paul was thankful for Euodia and Syntyche who did spiritual warfare on his behalf. Doris and I are equally thankful for I-1 intercessors such as Cathy and Alice who have taken many of the enemy's blows for us.

INTERCESSORS CHANGE ROLES

Because I am such a left-brained analytical person, I find myself very comfortable with categories like I-1 and I-2. I am aware that not all like to draw such lines. It is important to realize that even with the lines, God pushes intercessors back and forth across them as He chooses. Maybe the lines are not that important after all. Several of our I-2 intercessors have reported doing intense spiritual warfare as they prayed for us. And I am sure it has happened on many other occasions that we know nothing about because experienced intercessors will only share those experiences when and if God specifically gives them permission to do so. Much happens through them that we know nothing about.

A few years ago one of our I-2 intercessors was Cathryn Hoellwarth, then a member of our Sunday School class, but who since has moved away. I was away on a ministry trip and Cathryn was attending the Sunday evening service at the Anaheim Vineyard Fellowship where John Wimber pastors. It just so happened that Doris was sitting two rows in front of her. As Cathryn looked at Doris, she got a picture of my head surrounded by black, oppressive clouds. She began interceding for me, believing that it was a life-and-death struggle.

Later in the week, Cathryn discovered that I had been on a

flight to Detroit and, for some unknown reason, had blacked out on the plane. The paramedics and ambulance were waiting for me in Detroit, but after a thorough examination they could find nothing wrong and released me. I called Cathy Schaller the next day from Detroit and asked her if she had been praying for me. She said she had felt no special urgency to pray at that time. Apparently God had chosen to call Cathryn to stand in the gap for that assignment. Cathryn says, "I suppose God taps into the I-2 intercessors when the I-1 intercessors aren't available." What a comforting thought!

FILTERING OUT THE FLAKES

One of the most discussed chapters in Cindy Jacobs's excellent book *Possessing the Gates of the Enemy* is titled, "Flaky Intercession." She describes the flaky intercessors as "men and women who, for a variety of reasons, drift outside biblical guidelines in their zeal for prayer. They bring reproach on their ministries and confusion and division in the church."[3]

I have such a high regard for intercessors that I hate to think any could be less than angelic, but the reality is different as we saw in the story of Pastor Paul Freedman earlier in the chapter. Fortunately, we are talking about a minority, and as books such as Cindy's circulate, the minority I hope will become smaller and smaller.

Intercessors can and do appear on the scene for wrong motives. I have a list of six of them that Doris and I have used as a checklist for filtering out the flakes.

1. Bragging rights. Some intercessors derive great pleasure from bragging that "I am the one who prays for the pastor." The larger the church and the more inaccessible the pastor is to ordinary church members, the more acute is the temptation to do this bragging. The same will apply to any

Christian leader, especially those who have national and international visibility.

2. *A need for control*. This may be the most pernicious and pervasive characteristic of a flaky intercessor. We saw it clearly in the woman who prayed for Paul Freedman and caused disaster. Cindy Jacobs tells of "Estelle," whose prayer group "began to pray fervently that the pastor would 'see the light and get aligned with God'—which was synonymous with getting aligned with them." Estelle's mistake, Cindy says, was that "She felt that her 'revelations' were superior to what the pastor or elders heard from God."[4] She then goes on to explain how this tendency can be labeled as an "Absolom spirit." Need for control is very dangerous and should not be tolerated in a prayer partner if it ever arises.

3. *Lust or seduction*. It is sad but true that some women who may or may not be true intercessors are tempted by the lusts of the flesh. They are astute enough to recognize the prayer partner relationship as a potential pathway toward seduction. Most pastors have developed defense mechanisms against allowing this to happen in the counseling relationship, but some may be blindsided by trusted prayer partners. One woman tried this one on me, but fortunately she was not very good at it! In fact Doris sensed her intentions almost the moment she passed through her outer office into mine. This is not just a *little* flakiness; it is a *lot!*

4. *Sentimentalism*. "Praying for our pastor would be a lovely thing to do. I would love to try this. I think I could help the pastor so much by praying regularly." Statements like this reflect a low level of understanding of intercession in general, and wrong motives in particular.

5. *Pride*. Wrongly motivated intercessors are not able to handle the joy and spiritual stimulation that come from hearing from God and praying His will into being through the pastor. Consequently they think more highly of themselves than they ought to think. Almost all recognized intercessors have had battles with pride within themselves, and most are on guard against it constantly. Whenever pride raises its ugly head, they immediately confess it and tear down the stronghold. Some seek help from other intercessors. But sadly some do fall prey to spiritual pride. It comes out in many ways, one of the most destructive being a tendency to gossip about the pastor or about inside details of the ministry.

6. *Personal emotional needs*. The ministry of intercession seems to be a magnet for emotionally disturbed people. Prayer leaders are well aware of this and they have developed ways and means of handling these people without further compounding their emotional problems. But when they also seek personal relationships as prayer partners, the dangers are obvious. Those who think, "If I can only be the pastor's prayer partner, I'll be healed," need to search for other more viable forms of therapy.

I do not enjoy thinking about or writing about the deficiencies of intercessors. I much prefer to describe their positive characteristics as I will in the next chapter.

■ REFLECTION QUESTIONS ■

1. Discuss the story of Paul Freedman. How can his near-tragic mistake be avoided? > *Other gifts too*
2. How would you respond to a pastor's invitation for you to become an I-3 intercessor? How about an I-2?
3. There is a difference of opinion as to whether I-2 intercessors should be recruited or just specifically called by God to pray for the leader. What do you think?
4. Review and discuss the three parts of Cindy Jacobs's formula for recruiting intercessors.

1/ Wagner in a cong. setting how would he recruit what initiatives

5. Without mentioning names, give some concrete examples of some who have used the wrong motives mentioned toward the end of the chapter.

Notes
1. Cindy Jacobs, *Possessing the Gates of the Enemy* (Tarrytown, NY: Chosen Books, 1991), pp. 163,164.
2. Ibid., p. 159.
3. Ibid., p. 126.
4. Ibid., p. 126, 127.

A Profile of Personal Intercessors

IN THE NOT-TOO-DISTANT PAST I WOULD NOT HAVE BEEN able to explain what a personal intercessor was. Over the last few years, however, I have come to realize they are the elite in the Kingdom of God. They are the green berets, the Phi Beta Kappas, the Olympic teams of God's community. In fact soon after forming my own team of personal prayer partners I went through a period when I was both intimidated by the intercessors and envious of them.

I recall one particular morning when I was struggling with this matter before God in prayer. I said, "Father, please give me intimacy with you like I am seeing in these intercessors. I want to be like them."

Then came one of those moments that are few and far between for me, but daily bread for true intercessors, when I clearly heard God speaking to me in response to my petition. He first told me to take my pencil and draw three steps, which I promptly did.

God then showed me that the intercessors are on the top step, and I am on the middle step. Multitudes are on the bottom step. He said that the intercessors are too high to reach down and help many who are on the bottom step. He told me that He wanted me to be one of His middle-step people who are in close touch with the intercessors, but who also will help many people move up the stairway. He said that many whom I do help from the lower step to the middle step will then move on and pass me.

I sensed that I heard God say my task was not to minister in His throne room, but to be outside the throne room helping others to come nearer. Those who are already in the throne room will be a major link in bringing me closer to God.

God assured me that I do have clear access to Him. He affirmed the priesthood of all believers. Access to Him is not the question, but the degree of intimacy is. He showed me that His family is large and that He loves all His children. His perfect desire and calling for each child is to be in the place where they will be the greatest blessing to all. Not all of His children are as yet in the place He wants them, but He seemed to assure me that I was in exactly the place where I was supposed to be, and that I was to rejoice in it rather than to fret over it.

I realize I do not always hear God as clearly as I should, but I believe that was one of the times I did. I was greatly relieved. Not that I wouldn't like to be an intercessor—I would. I would also like to be a guitar player, an airplane pilot, a major league shortstop, just to name a few. But that is not who I am. Knowing that I am not an intercessor helps me relate to intercessors all the more creatively.

THE PROFILE

I now know enough intercessors and know them well enough to see a profile emerging. Not that every intercessor would score a "10" on each one of the items, but when the cumulative total is added up, they will score higher than most people. Because of the nature of this particular book, the profile is naturally biased toward personal intercessors rather than general intercessors or crisis intercessors, but in general it will apply to all.

The Gift of Intercession

When God calls members of His family to a certain task or ministry, He provides them with the supernatural gifting to accomplish it according to His will. For those He has called to the upper step or into the throne room as intercessors, He has provided what I like to call the spiritual gift of intercession. I described this concept in detail in chapter 2, indicating there that those with the gift of intercession ordinarily pray from two to five hours a day. The only exceptions I have found are working mothers with young families who would pray more than two hours if they could, but truly cannot carve the time out of their schedules. Even so, they rarely let a day go by without praying at least one hour.

I was comforted not too long ago when I learned I was not the first to suggest something we can regard as a legitimate spiritual gift of intercession. None other than St. John Chrysostom of the fourth century saw it also. In his commentary on Romans he mentions the gifts of prophecy, wisdom, healings, miracles, tongues, and then says, "There was also a gift of prayer...and he who had this prayed for all the people." He said that those who had the gift were known by much interceding to God, many mental groanings, falling before God, and "asking the things that were profitable for all."[1]

The two chief characteristics I have seen of those with the gift of intercession is that they love to pray and they see the results of their intercession.

Spiritual gifts frequently come in mixes, and certain pairings of gifts are very common such as pastor and teacher. Many of those I know with the gift of intercession also have been given spiritual gifts of prophecy (including what some call "word of knowledge") and discernment of spirits. Whether this is true across the board I do not know, although I would not be surprised if it is.

Close Relationship to God

I like the way my friend Evelyn Christenson describes her prayer time. She says it is no longer a "grocery list" of a few minutes of praise and intercession as it used to be. "I've learned that my closet prayer time involves so much of His replenishing my emotional needs—with God and I exchanging our mutual love. There's much more listening on my part than before." Evelyn speaks for many intercessors when she says, "My average day starts at 4:30 a.m. and I spend several hours alone with the Lord almost every day." Her last resort, "threadbare" time, is two hours.[2]

All Christians have a desire to be close to God. But the honest truth is that for the majority of Christians the time set aside for prayer is relatively short and the actual feelings of closeness to God during those times is not, for the most part, all that we hear the intercessors describing. Intercessors are not just average Christians any more than evangelists or pastors or prophets or teachers are. Part of their difference from others is not how many lost souls they lead to Christ, but their intimate relationship with the Father.

Relatively few would feel that their life goals were being fulfilled by spending 10 hours a day in prayer 365 days a year as do the Sisters of Perpetual Adoration in Anchorage, Alaska. One correctly says, "Many cannot understand our lifestyle, not even many of our families." Then she explains, "But for us, this has brought us very close to God, and fulfills our potential."[3]

Historically, one of the most famous intercessors is Julian of Norwich who spent her life as an "anchoress," cloistering herself alone for prayer in the early fifteenth century. Her memory remains mainly because of her book, *Sixteen Revelations of Divine Love,* which profoundly describes her closeness to God. She directed her thoughts to those who "deliberately choose God in this life for love"; people she called "the little and the simple." For a shortened version of her book she uses the

---

Openness and obedience are keys to hearing from God.

---

meaningful title *Comfortable Words for Christ's Lovers.*[4] The deep closeness of intercessors to the Father apparently has not changed much at least over the past 600 years.

Receive Words from God

An important part of what happens when intercessors spend long periods of time in very close relationship to God is that they hear directly from Him. My friend David Bryant, leader of the dynamic Concerts of Prayer movement, calls this the "strategy of silence." In the strategy of silence we go before God to seek His direction even in what we should pray about and how we should pray.

Openness and obedience are keys to hearing from God. At times the instructions God gives are almost as unconventional as when He told Ezekiel to eat a scroll or lie on his left side for 390 days or shave his head and beard and burn one-third of his hair in the middle of the city (Ezek. 4–5). But intercessors anointed for this strategy of silence have developed the discernment to know when it is authentic.

A few years ago I was doing a church-planting seminar in Toronto. I called Cathy Schaller on Tuesday and she prayed for me on the phone. She sensed that God wanted to use me to "release gifts of healing." This was hard to understand because it had nothing to do with the subject of the seminar, nor was I in the habit, as some of my friends are, of praying to release gifts in others. My understanding of spiritual gifts is a bit more conservative than that and Cathy knew it. She indicated that God would show me what to do the next day, Wednesday.

I expected He would show me what to do in my prayer time, but I got nothing. Meanwhile, Joseph Mak, one of our Fuller graduates, had called Doris a week previously asking her if I would pray for two sick people, one in the hospital, when I went to Toronto. I was reluctant because I ordinarily do not do that, but I sensed God wanted me to do it this time so I agreed. When I arrived in Toronto, Joseph Mak said that God had used the telephone call to Doris as the turning point in the sickness of Anisa, the woman in the hospital, and that she had been discharged. We then agreed to pray at the hotel Wednesday afternoon.

Anisa was late for the appointment, but the other woman I was to pray for, Rita, was there with her pastor. Her finger had been damaged in a badminton game, but when I asked her about it she said she was already healed. I said how? She said, "I prayed and God healed me." When I told her this was really unusual, she said it had happened to her many times. Then I asked her if she prays for healing for others. She said, "No, I wouldn't dare. I have only told one other person about this other than you." By then I knew she had a gift of healing and I told her so. "No, not me," she protested, "I'm not a doctor like you."

Before we left, Rita prayed both for Anisa and her pastor and saw God's healing power manifested. I then prayed that God would release the gift of healing in Rita, and exhorted her to begin to use it, holding herself accountable to her pastor and Joseph Mak.

So far as I can recall, this is the only time I have ever ministered in this way. My point is this: The indication that this incident was God's will came through an intercessor who was accustomed to practicing the strategy of silence and discerning the will of God.

Who is Everett? During the period of time when our I-1 baton was being passed from Cathy Schaller to Alice Smith, Alice called me early one morning. I was in the midst of teaching a one-week intensive Doctor of Ministry course. She said that morning (Houston is two hours ahead of us) God had told her there was a pastor named Everett in my class who was going through a difficult time in his life and whom God wanted to minister to.

When I got to class, sure enough, Everett Briard, pastor of a Presbyterian Church in Canada, responded with total astonishment, almost unbelief, that such a thing could happen. We as a class prayed for him, and some other pastors ministered to him personally as well. He testified to us that he had felt a definite change in his spiritual and mental outlook.

Nine months later, Everett wrote a letter to me telling me how important Alice's word had become to him. "I had been struggling with many things for a long time," he said, "not the least of which was the inability to get rid of an underlying sense of meaninglessness, and periodic times of degrees of depression." He said that in a seminar two weeks after the word from Alice he had heard a Christian psychologist say that only through therapy could a person be moved from low self-esteem and self-hate to high self-esteem.

But, Everett said, "God did that for me instantly during your class. He set me free and has given me a sense of newness in ministry. Things which used to throw me into deep despondency no longer have the power to do that. I am so grateful."

You can imagine how grateful I am as well, seeing God use me as a relatively passive instrument to link a Houston intercessor with a Canadian pastor visiting in Pasadena, California, and observe God's power manifested in a mighty way. Yes, intercessors do hear from God.

Prophetic Intercession

All true intercessors hear from God on a regular basis and most from time to time will move into prophetic intercession. For some, prophetic intercession is an ongoing ministry under their gift of intercession. Don Bloch, a lay minister from Jacksonville, Florida, is an example of one who has a ministry of prophetic intercession. He prays on call from the Lord for situations all over the world.

Bloch says, "The Lord shows me events that are about to take place and asks me to pray for them. I believe God is calling many people to be intercessors and more and more He is giving the gift of prophetic intercession."[5]

Cindy Jacobs defines prophetic intercession as "an urging to pray given by the Holy Spirit for situations or circumstances about which you have very little knowledge in the natural. You pray for the prayer requests that are on the heart of God."[6]

Lois Main, an intercessor from Coalinga, California, could not sleep one night in April 1983. She sensed she heard the Lord say, "Pray for the people of Coalinga. Go out and pray now."

Although it was a strange time for such an assignment, Lois obeyed, got dressed, and walked the dark and deserted streets of Coalinga faithfully, praying for the people in each building she passed. After a long period of time, she felt the release to go back to bed and sleep the rest of the night.

The next afternoon Coalinga suffered a 6.5 earthquake. The local hospital was braced and on high alert to treat all the victims. However, only 25 people showed up, most for minor injuries.

Sondra Johnson, who tells this story, comments, "Intercessors must be willing to step out in faith and pray as God speaks to their hearts. Like most who pray prophetically, we might never know the results. But we must leave that to God, knowing we have done His will."[7] Lois Main had the added satisfaction of knowing the results.

Quiet People

Although there are several notable exceptions to this, the great majority of intercessors are quiet people. They do not like to be

---

For personal intercessors, as over against other kinds of intercessors, the pastor or other leader they have been called to pray for is usually elevated to a high priority in the total prayer schedule.

---

up front. They do not desire their names to be widely known. Even some who have written books on intercession would prefer their names be left off the book, but they somewhat reluctantly bow to the wisdom of editors and publishers who know the book will be more widely distributed with the name than without it.

Colleen Townsend Evans says that "aloneness" is one of the prices intercessors regularly pay. "As an intercessor," she says, "be prepared to spend some very quiet alone hours." Other people will not always know or even understand what an intercessor is praying about. Evans says intercessors "will be put in quiet corners where no one will know what we are doing, and God will seal our lips so that we are not to boast or talk about what we are doing."[8]

The apostle Paul might have had intercessors in mind when

he said, "Those members of the body which seem to be weaker are necessary. And those members of the body which we think to be less honorable, on these we bestow greater honor" (1 Cor. 12:22,23). Although we may not see them much, the Body of Christ needs intercessors for a healthy life just as much as our physical body needs a pituitary gland, which we see even less.

The Pastor Has a High Priority

For personal intercessors, as over against other kinds of intercessors, the pastor or other leader they have been called to pray for is usually elevated to a high priority in the total prayer schedule. It does not happen every day, but it is not unusual for Doris and me to get reports that one of our intercessors has prayed for us one hour or even several hours on a particular day. We only hear about those occasions when the prayer partner has been released by God to tell us, which I am sure is only a fraction of the times it happens. Sometimes we will know exactly why they prayed, sometimes we never know.

One of the times of special intercession, among many I did know, was on a Sunday evening when Cathy Schaller was ironing in her kitchen. At 6:30 the Holy Spirit came on her for intercession and she prayed for me until she was released at 7:00 P.M. Then she went back to her ironing and called me the next morning to see why she had prayed.

That Sunday evening Doris and I had gone to Anaheim Vineyard, and before the service, we dropped in at Pastor John Wimber's office to have a Coke with John and his wife, Carol. As we chatted, I told him of a case the preceding week where I had been privileged to pray for a six-year-old boy who had been born with no ears. Miraculously, the ears started to grow a half hour after the prayer session.

When John heard the story, he spontaneously asked me to share the testimony with the congregation. To say the least, I was not prepared to speak to 3,000 people about an incident so dramatic that I myself had not had time to process it, while focusing attention on the power of God, not myself, and drawing out an application for the congregation.

But the sharing went well, the congregation was blessed, and I believe God was glorified. Thanks to Cathy's priorities. I spoke that evening, of course, between 6:30 and 7:00.

Because of these priorities, it is imperative that the potential intercessor be totally honest when considering a request to become a prayer partner. Assigning high priority does not imply exclusivity. I have mentioned that several of our prayer partners have been assigned more than one leader for intercession, and that the intensity of prayer for each can vary over time.

Mary Lance Sisk, for instance, also prays for Leighton Ford and Joni Eareckson Tada. For others it does mean they are to pray for only one at a time. This is why I was pleased that Lil Walker was honest in turning down my first invitation to become a prayer partner because she had been assigned Paul Cedar. At the same time, Mary Wernle did agree to pray for me and for years, although she prays for many people, the bulk of her personal prayer time has been focused on Doris and me.

Open Communication

Personal intercessors maintain open communication channels with the pastor for whom they are praying. That is why it is necessary for both the leader and the intercessor to be aware of the prayer partner relationship. Secret prayer partners undoubtedly have some value, but at least one study done by Nancy Pfaff has shown that it is limited.

Knowing explicitly about the prayer partner agreement opens the way to a covenant relationship in which each side can understand and agree upon mutual responsibilities. Some of the ingredients for such a relationship and some suggestions to keep the communication flowing will come in the next chapter.

The duration of the relationship of a prayer partner to the pastor is usually indefinite. As I have mentioned previously, I think it is best to assume from the start that it will be a long-term arrangement. Nothing is intrinsically wrong with recruiting an intercessor for six months or a year, but an open-ended agreement is more in order. Many intercessors feel their assignment is for a lifetime, but circumstances may change on both sides and God may direct that the relationship be changed.

Nancy Pfaff, for example, feels she is a combination of crisis and personal intercessor. Her first assignment was to Dan Reeves, a prominent church growth consultant. After some years she was released as an I-1 intercessor for Dan, but continues as an I-2 or I-3. Her new I-1 assignment is as staff intercessor for Church Resource Ministries where she prays especially for Sam Metcalf, Bob Logan, Steve Ogne and Joan Florio.

My point is that questions regarding ending one assignment and moving on to another cannot be adequately dealt with unless there is open communication between the pastor and the intercessor.

Confidentiality

When Cindy Jacobs lists the qualifications of personal prayer partners, number two on her list (after a commitment to pray) is confidentiality.[9] Because I received my initial prayer partners from people with whom I had developed a relationship over a long period of time, confidentiality did not at first occur to me as an important consideration.

I clearly recall when I approached Bobbye Byerly about praying for us, she emphasized more than once that what we shared as prayer requests would be kept strictly confidential and we could totally depend on it. She said she had known of cases where this had been violated and personal prayer requests had become subjects of gossip, doing much damage to people and their ministries.

Fortunately, Doris and I did not have to go through any bad experiences to learn how important confidentiality is, but since then we have found ourselves sharing items with I-1 and I-2 intercessors that were definitely not for public knowledge. And we have felt our shared information was as secure as the papers we have in our safe deposit box in the bank. Only with this assurance can pastors and other leaders open up their deeper and most urgent needs to the intercessors.

Seasons of Dryness

It would be easy to put intercessors up on such a spiritual pedestal that we forget they are human just like the rest of us. But they themselves will be the first to remind us of their frailty. Intercessors have their ups and downs. They have their good days and their bad days. They can leave a powerful mountaintop experience with God and plunge into the valley. One of our roles as leaders is to understand this and nurture them through difficult periods just as they do with us.

A while ago Alice Smith went through a particularly strenuous time of intercession and spiritual warfare in Israel where she felt that significant battles were won against some high-ranking principalities. Soon after that she wrote to Doris and me saying, "I am in the midst of a very difficult time of dryness before the Lord. This is not uncommon to experience because intercessors have to have a spiritual 'tune up' every once in a while to see if they are praying for the benefits, or really praying and enjoying the Lord because of who He is." Here again is the heart of a true intercessor who has no greater desire than a close relationship with God.

"Especially after a very high spiritual experience such as I encountered in Israel," Alice says, "there is often the tendency to press into the Lord for a 'bigger high,' while He is more interested in the quiet, still fellowship of knowing His presence." She seemed somewhat apologetic that even when she prayed for us, she was not hearing much from the Lord. She was apologetic, that is, to us, but certainly not to the Lord who, she felt, was monitoring her faithfulness at that point. She concludes by saying, "These times always spark a fresh gratitude for when I do hear Him speak once again."

Soon afterward, as we knew and she knew would happen, the dry period ended and things returned to normal. Meanwhile, we noticed during that period God had given extra assignments to some I-2 intercessors. For example, during that time Doris and I made a very significant visit to the March for Jesus office in London and, as I mentioned previously, Dave Rumph and Bobbye Byerly were used by the Lord in a special way to pray the event into being.

Need Help from Others

From time to time I have mentioned the Aarons and Hurs whom God sends to support the intercessors in times of need. Sometimes they receive spontaneous, one-time assignments. But some intercessors themselves have recruited ongoing teams of prayer partners.

Alice Smith, for example, has a very active prayer partners team, many of whom also have a gift of intercession. Thirteen of them have become I-3 intercessors for Doris and me. When Alice went to Israel and subsequently through the "dry time" described above, she assigned her prayer partners to stand in the gap for me, which they did. Since then, Alice has forwarded several notes they wrote to her expressing what they thought they were hearing about us. A typical note reads, "The Lord has continued this past week to speak to me about Mr. Wagner. The following four words have come to me for whatever confirmation or invitation they may contain..."

Many intercessors do not intuitively realize they need permanent prayer partners just as much as other leaders do. Years ago when we were just beginning to learn about personal intercession and all that was involved in it, Christy Graham, who is normally a crisis intercessor, received a longer term assignment to be a personal intercessor for Cathy Schaller. God told her that Cathy absorbs many of the attacks of the enemy that would otherwise get through to me and that she herself needed more protection. When Christy told Cathy that she was to pray for her, Cathy's initial reaction was, "Pray for *me?* Why do I need prayer? Is there something wrong with me?"

So Christy responded, "Well, what's wrong with Peter? Why does he need prayer?" Cathy immediately saw the point and welcomed Christy as a prayer partner. I was interested that God never did assign Christy as a prayer partner for me, but only for Cathy.

Evelyn Christenson, a premier intercessor, suggests that intercessors pair off for mutual prayer support. She says, "Do you have someone who will pray for you and for whom you will pray?...Find one person with whom you can share the secret problems and needs of your life. Someone who cares and who will never, never divulge your secrets. Then fulfill the law of Christ by 'bearing one another's burdens' (see Gal. 6:2)."[10]

THE REWARDS

If I did not know better, I would be embarrassed at seeing the power of God flow through my ministry, knowing full well that a major reason for this is the faithful intercession of my precious and faithful prayer partners. I am the one who gets praised; I am the one who gets the honors; I am the one who gets paid for it. But none of the above ordinarily comes to the prayer partners. Nor do the intercessors desire any of those rewards. One of the things my prayer partners are constantly praying for is that my ministry will bear great fruit primarily in the lives of others, but as that happens I get the credit. And they are delighted.

Joshua got the credit for being the general who defeated Amalek and won the battle of Rephidim. But the divine power to do it came through Moses' intercession. Joshua won and Moses was also delighted.

We need to understand, however, that intercessors do feel they are amply rewarded for their ministry. I believe their greatest reward awaits them in heaven. If believers in heaven are in concentric circles around God's throne, the intercessors will be in the middle, right behind the 24 elders and the 4 living creatures.

In the here and now, a substantial reward for intercessors is to watch their prayers birth the purposes of God in the lives and ministries of the pastors for whom they are praying. Experienced intercessors see many things happening in their churches that even the pastors have no idea they are praying through. It is a true thrill for the intercessors.

But the consistent testimony I get from intercessors is that by far their greatest reward is their close relationship with the Father. More than most Christians ever do, they experience the fullness of the love of God day in and day out.

HOW TO PRAY FOR PASTORS

I own several prayer guides for leaders, prepared by mature intercessors. As I examine them, I discover that personal intercessors have reached a general consensus about what to pray for. The guides presuppose that the intercessor has moved into the presence of God through worship and praise; they have a close communion with the Father; and their prayers are consistent with the Word of God. The manuals also state that they should not be regarded as formulas for prayer, but as outlines that should be used with the flow of the Holy Spirit.

The **guide** I find most helpful was prepared by one of our 12 intercessors, Elizabeth Alves, president of Intercessors International. It is found in the chapter of her book *Becoming* *a Prayer Warrior* called "Daily Prayers." Each day lists a topic with subtopics, Scripture passages and written prayers. According to the way God is leading, intercessors will use any or all of the three categories. Beth Alves's desire is to provide an aid so that intercessors can "be obedient and faithful in 'standing in the gap' on behalf of missionaries, ministers, and spiritual leaders assigned for prayer."[11] Her general outline goes as follows:

> **Sunday:** Favor with God (spiritual revelation, anointing, holiness).
> **Monday:** Favor with others (congregations, ministry staff, unsaved).
> **Tuesday:** Increased vision (wisdom and enlightenment, motives, guidance).
> **Wednesday:** Spirit, Soul, Body (health, appearance, attitudes, spiritual and physical wholeness).
> **Thursday:** Protection (temptation, deception, enemies).
> **Friday:** Finances (priorities, blessings).
> **Saturday:** Family (general, spouse, children).

I like what Will Bruce says in his brochure, "Pastors Need Prayer, Too," "No matter how well you pay your pastor, praise him or work for him, it is only through earnest, strategic prayer that you can ever really help him be an effective minister in the hands of almighty God."[12]

■ REFLECTION QUESTIONS ■

1. Do you know one or more people you would regard as having the gift of intercession? Talk about them.
2. Look once again at Peter Wagner's image of the three steps. Where would you locate yourself?
3. Do you believe that God really speaks as specifically as

telling Alice Smith about Everett? Has it ever happened to you?

4. What are some of the reasons why intercessors need others to pray for them?
5. Using the daily prayer outline at the end of the chapter, spend a few minutes praying for your pastor by touching on all the categories mentioned.

Notes

1. Philip Schaff, ed., *A Select Library of the Nicene and Post Nicene Fathers of the Christian Church,* Vol. XI: Saint Chrysostom (Grand Rapids, MI: Wm. Eerdmans Publishing Company, 1956), p. 447.
2. Judith Couchman, "The High Cost of Prayer: An Interview with Evelyn Christenson," *Christian Life,* January 1987, p. 12.
3. Charles Hillinger, "Isolated in Anchorage Cloister, Nuns Say They Feel Closer to God," *Los Angeles Times,* December 23, 1989, p. S4.
4. J. Walsh, "Julian of Norwich," *New Catholic Encyclopedia,* Vol. VIII (New York, NY: McGraw-Hill Book Company, 1967), pp. 48, 49.
5. Barbara White, "Called to Prophetic Intercession," *The Breakthrough Intercessor,* January-February 1991, p. 5.
6. Cindy Jacobs, *Possessing the Gates of the Enemy* (Tarrytown, NY: Chosen Books, 1991), pp. 146,147.
7. Sondra Johnson, "Obeying the Call," *The Breakthrough Intercessor,* January-February 1991, p. 4.
8. Colleen Townsend Evans, "The Cost of Intercession," *Breakthrough,* July/August 1989, p. 1.
9. Jacobs, *Possessing the Gates,* p. 164.
10. Evelyn Christenson, *What Happens When Women Pray* (Wheaton, IL: Victor Books, 1975), p. 100.
11. Elizabeth Alves, *Becoming a Prayer Warrior* (Ventura, CA: Renew Books, 1998), pp 167-210.
12. Will Bruce, "Pastors Need Prayer, Too" (Overseas Missionary Fellowship, 404 S. Church Street, Robesonia, PA 19551 215-693-5881).

Maintaining Your Intercessors

THE APOSTLE PAUL VALUED PERSONAL INTERCESSION HIGH-
ly. He requested it in several of his epistles, but none
in more detail than the epistle to the Ephesians. The
church at Ephesus was born out of some of the most
intense spiritual warfare of Paul's entire career. In Ephesus, Paul had dealt with spiritual forces of darkness on
every level; from evil spirits being cast out through
handkerchiefs that were taken from him, to dealing with
the seven sons of Sceva, to burning magical parapher-
nalia, to Diana of the Ephesians who was known as the
territorial spirit over the whole region.

This is why Paul deals so much with topics such as
spiritual warfare and the armor of God in his epistle.
Clinton E. Arnold observes that Ephesians contains "a
substantially higher concentration of power terminology
than any other epistle attributed to Paul."[1] A weapon of
spiritual warfare to which Paul gives a high profile is

prayer. He says, "Praying always with all prayer and supplication in the Spirit" (Eph. 6:18). Powerful prayer is necessary for intense spiritual warfare.

INTERCESSION PROTECTS US

I see two specific lines of protection "against principalities, against powers, against the rulers of the darkness of this age, against spiritual hosts of wickedness in the heavenly places" (Eph. 6:12) that Paul addresses. The first is our individual protection, the whole armor of God (Eph. 6:11-17). Each one of us has the responsibility to put on the whole armor of God day by day. Pastors and other Christian leaders who fail to do this either through ignorance or indifference make themselves unnecessarily vulnerable to "the fiery darts of the wicked one" (Eph. 6:16).

The second line of protection against the enemy is intercession. In my Bible version, *(New King James Version)* the prayer passage beginning with Ephesians 6:18 is separated from the last verse of the whole armor of God passage, verse 17, by only a semicolon. Prayer is not simply a polite and appropriate closing formality in the epistle of Ephesians, but it is an integral component of the weapons of spiritual warfare.

Paul requests, first of all, general intercession, which he calls "supplication for all the saints" (Eph. 6:18). Second, he becomes much more personal and asks them to pray "for me" (Eph. 6:19).

He does not stop in this instance with a rather vague request for prayer as he does when writing to the Thessalonians: "Brethren, pray for us" (1 Thess. 5:25). Rather, he wants the Ephesians specifically to pray "that utterance may be given to me, that I may open my mouth boldly to make known the mystery of the gospel" (Eph. 6:19).

Here we see Paul as the leader requesting his personal intercessors to pray for effectiveness in his ministry. Paul's ministry was essentially evangelistic. He was a cross-cultural church planter. His primary task was to make known the gospel. Other leaders have other primary ministries according to their spiritual gifts.

Timothy, Priscilla and Aquila, Luke, Titus, John Mark, Philemon and others of Paul's colleagues and associates had min-

---

To the degree the intercessors pray, the leaders gain protection against the fiery darts of the wicked one, over and above the whole armor of God they are responsible for using.

---

istries different from Paul's. Their personal intercessors would have focused on other kinds of ministry. I, for example, am a leader with a very marginal evangelistic ministry and my intercessors rarely have prayed for me as Paul's prayed for him. But the principle is the same. The prayer partners pray for the leader's ministry whatever it might be.

To the degree our intercessors pray for us, we gain protection against the fiery darts of the wicked one, over and above the whole armor of God we ourselves are responsible for using.

LEADERS DO RECEIVE INTERCESSION

I do not want to give the impression that because personal intercession for leaders is underutilized, it is not utilized at all. I wrote a letter to 35 celebrity leaders whose names are household words in the American evangelical community and was pleasantly surprised to find that 28 of them could name people who pray for them on a regular basis. At least 19 of these would be I-1 intercessors by the definition I am using, figuring out to 54 percent. Frankly, I believe the 54 percent is a bit high because of the select list I wrote to. If my hypotheses are correct, one of the reasons God has been able to give them positions of visibility and influence is because they were utilizing personal prayer partners.

A couple of interesting facts emerged from the survey. One was that the age of the intercessors seemed disproportionately high. A large number are in their 60s or above. Perhaps a combination of Christian maturity and retirement from vocational careers increases the eligibility and availability of many for serious intercession.

The other fact was that one half of those who could name their intercessors named other family members: spouses, parents, grandparents and grown children.

Although James Dobson did not happen to be on the list I wrote to, his biography, *Dr. Dobson: Turning Hearts Toward Home*, reveals that he depends greatly on personal prayer partners. Two are mentioned. One is his wife, Shirley, who says that when they almost lost their children four times during a six-month period, she came under a great burden of prayer. Recognizing this as an attack of Satan, she says, "To counteract this, I bathed our children and Jim in prayer. I still spend one day a week fasting and praying for them."[2]

Dobson's other prayer partner is Nobel Hathaway, 71, a personal friend of James Dobson's parents. A widower, Hathaway says, "I have committed my remaining days to continue the ministry of prayer that Dr. Dobson's parents started. Every morning before breakfast, I have a one-man prayer meeting for Jim, Shirley, Danae, and Ryan. I am committed to bombarding the skies with prayers for the Dobsons."[3]

Reinhard Bonnke, one of today's foremost crusade evangelists, has a ministry akin to that of the apostle Paul. Like Paul, he depends heavily on intercession. My friend Suzette Hattingh serves not only as Bonnke's I-1 intercessor, but she also mobilizes massive prayer for each crusade. Before Bonnke preaches, Suzette will have gathered thousands in a given city, instructing and releasing them for true intercession. Bonnke says, "It is not a case of singing choruses and praying for a blessing, but of pulling down the strongholds of Satan. Intercessors are a mighty battering ram."[4]

THE RESPONSIBILITY OF THE PASTORS

There may be exceptions, but intercession is not usually generated and sustained spontaneously. Pastors and other leaders must be open to receive intercession and to encourage their intercessors.

I was shocked to learn that some years ago Reinhard Bonnke called in Suzette Hattingh and said, "At least five of the leading pastors of this nation have warned me not to form an intercession department in Christ for All Nations because of problems they told me they experienced with their personal and general intercessors!" I am glad to report that Bonnke was not deterred from establishing a ministry of intercession, but nevertheless he asked Hattingh to investigate.

Suzette visited each personal intercessor of each of the concerned pastors. She found that they were frustrated, discouraged and disappointed because their pastors did not understand their responsibility as leaders. The intercessors agreed that there were four basic problems:

1. Lack of information
2. Lack of input and trust from the pastors
3. Lack of feedback on answered prayers

4. Lack of openness between intercessors and leadership.

Since then Suzette Hattingh has had personal contact with thousands of serious intercessors. She says, "I have found the problems mentioned above among all levels of intercessors."[5]

Very frequently when a ministry of personal intercession breaks down, the leader is at fault. When leaders are distant and indifferent toward their intercessors, many prayer warriors will eventually lay down their weapons, and both the leader and the intercessor come short of what God wants them to be.

MAINTAINING THE INTERCESSORS

In his concluding paragraph of Ephesians 6, Paul provides us with what I consider a model of how we as leaders should relate to our intercessors in order to maintain their interest and their faithfulness to do spiritual warfare on our behalf. By this I do not mean to imply that their primary motivation is anything other than their desire to serve God and obey Him. If God has called intercessors to pray for us, He will help maintain them. But I also think that, in His providence, God also gives us a role in keeping the relationship alive and well.

Paul sensed this, I believe, when he told them he was sending Tychicus to them. Back in those days before telephones, faxes and express mail, the preferred way to communicate was by personal messenger. The messenger would often carry a letter, as Tychicus undoubtedly did in this case, but even the letter could not substitute for the personal words of the messenger.

What was Tychicus supposed to do when he met the intercessors? Two things:

- Share information. "That you may know our affairs" (Eph. 6:22).

- Share Paul's love and encouragement. "Comfort your hearts" (Eph. 6:22).

Personal prayer partners typically do not make high demands on the pastor they pray for. But they are extremely grateful if we provide for them the information they need to pray intelligently, and if we, from time to time, encourage them with words of appreciation for their ministry on our behalf.

Pray for Your Intercessors
The relationship between pastors and intercessors is not a mutual relationship. Receiving intercession is not like borrowing money that has to be repaid. Joshua won the battle because he received Moses' intercession and returned very little if any.

The term I have used throughout this book, "prayer partners," has also been used by some as describing a reciprocal relationship. "You pray for me and I'll pray for you." This is a very fruitful relationship. In the last chapter, I mentioned how Evelyn Christenson recommends it and how she needs at least one such relationship as an intercessor herself. However, this is not the sense in which I have been using "prayer partners" in this book.

If I tried to repay the prayer I receive from my prayer partners, I would do little other than pray. Attempting to do that would be just under attempting to repay Jesus for my redemption. Impossible! So I have learned to receive their prayers as a gift of God's grace and their obedience.

All this does not mean that we should take our prayer partners for granted. I thank God for our prayer partners every day. I keep a picture of each pasted inside the front cover of my Bible and I turn to the pictures and pray for each one by name. I do not usually spend a long time on each one, but I bring each before God's throne. In the epistle to the Ephesians in which Paul asks for intercession, he also says, "I...do not cease to give thanks for you, making mention of you in my prayers" (Eph. 1:15,16). This is what I try to do also.

There are occasions where I do pray more for my prayer partners. I often pray when I know that one of them is going through a particularly difficult time. I pray as well when they are part of an actual ministry involvement along with me. For example, I prayed a good bit for Bobbye Byerly and Mary Lance Sisk when they were gathering a team of intercessors who accompanied us to Argentina in 1991 for our first annual Harvest Evangelism International Institute. But, I must stress, during that period of time they were praying for me much more than I was praying for them.

Then we all intensified our prayers for each other when we discovered that a group of Argentine witches and warlocks had set up an "occult fair" in the same hotel we were using to claim the territory for Satan one week before and during the week of our institute. Because of the intercessors, the witches' chants, incantations, curses and attempts at infiltration were effectively neutralized. On the last day, the government expelled them from the hotel for illegally practicing divination, and a local newspaper ran a cartoon showing the witches flying out of the hotel on broomsticks. Shades of Ephesus! We know well why Paul so greatly desired intercession.

Communicate Regularly

Communicating is the part that takes time. One of the best known cases of missionary history where evangelism was stimulated through prayer occurred when J. O. Fraser recruited prayer partners for his evangelistic work among the Lisu of Burma. For years nothing happened outwardly as he preached the gospel, but inwardly he learned that the real battle he faced was a spiritual battle. He said, "I know enough about Satan to realize that he will have all his weapons ready for determined opposition. He would be a missionary simpleton who expected plain sailing in any work of God. I will not."[6]

Fraser then wrote home to his mother who for years had ministered as what we would call his I-1 intercessor. He asked his mother to recruit "a group of like-minded friends, whether few or many, whether in one place or scattered" to join with her in prayer for the Lisu. The results were dramatic. Hundreds of Lisu families came to Christ in a short period of time. But that is not the immediate point. The point is that when James Fraser requested her to find prayer partners he was wise enough also to say to his mother, "If you could form a small prayer circle, I would write regularly to the members."[7]

Fraser was very serious. He said, "I am not asking you just to give 'help' in prayer as a sort of sideline, but I am trying to roll the *main responsibility* of this prayer warfare on you. I want you to take the *burden* of these people on your shoulders. I want you to wrestle with God for them." And his role? He saw himself as an intelligence officer. "I shall feel more and more that a big responsibility rests on me to keep you well informed."[8] He was prepared to invest the time necessary to communicate with his prayer partners.

John Maxwell, from whom I learned most about personal prayer partners, gives communication with intercessors a high priority. The 100 men who pray for him have privileges that other church members do not have, particularly accessibility to the senior pastor. John does not send a Tychicus to them, but he meets with them personally four times a year, three times for breakfast and once on an all-day prayer partner retreat where they eat together, play together, learn together and above all pray together. He meets with one-fourth of them every Sunday morning before the service on a rotating basis. He shares his needs, and they lay on hands and pray God's anointing on their leader. John has lunch once a month with his I-1 intercessor, Bill Klassen.

Because my intercessors are scattered around the country, I do not find it as easy to keep in contact with them as I might if they were in the same church. By this I do not mean that it is easy for John Maxwell, either. He invests an enormous amount of his time and energy in keeping in touch with them. Doris and I were frustrated about how to communicate with the I-3 intercessors until Jane Rumph, who is one of our original I-2 prayer partners, agreed to become the prayer coordinator for our ministry. Jane keeps the mailing list of more than 100 up to date and is in personal contact with several of them. When we put off writing for too long, Jane gets on our case, as we have instructed her to do.

Letters to Intercessors

Doris and I periodically write a long letter to our I-1 and I-2 intercessors. We are very open and honest with them. When major decisions need to be made, they are the first to know and they pray us through them.

None was more important than the decision we made to coordinate the United Prayer Track of the A.D. 2000 movement, which they all were praying about. As they prayed with us for weeks and even months, they began hearing clearly from the Lord that the A.D. 2000 movement was a major item on the heart of God for the 1990s, and that the invitation to be a part of it was a call from Him. As much as anything else, these divine assurances through our prayer partners convinced us that God wanted us to make this high-level commitment, which has had radical implications for our future ministry.

When we write that letter, we always include our ministry itinerary for the next few weeks so they know exactly where we are and what we are doing. We also enclose copies of vital correspondence on issues we are dealing with, reports I write or receive, photocopies of crucial articles and the like. Jane Rumph types this letter and mails it to the I-1 and I-2 prayer partners. Then she edits it to make it shorter and to remove the sensitive material and sends the edited version along with the itinerary to the I-3 intercessors.

This obviously requires considerably more effort than we had to expend in the days when our prayer partners were all members of our Sunday School class. Then I would talk to Cathy Schaller on the phone two or three times a week, and

---

The devil attacks the relationship of a pastor and intercessors in three principal areas: spiritual dependency, emotional dependency and physical dependency.

---

see them all every Sunday morning. I formed the habit, which I still maintain, of being sure that I personally greet and give a hug to each one of our prayer partners who is there on Sunday morning and let them know I love and appreciate them. As Cindy Jacobs says, "People need to be thanked often for their prayer sacrifice. They work hard at this."[9]

When a particular need arises, Doris or I will call our out-of-town prayer partners on an individual basis. Jane Rumph is also tooled to initiate a prayer chain when the whole team is needed for urgent prayer. She phones those who are out of town and Joanna McClure contacts the locals.

Most of the time, however, the seven prayer partners who live in other parts of the country are the ones who initiate telephone conversations with us. Sometimes they do it simply because it has been a long time since we have talked. Other times they call with a fresh word they have received from the Lord concerning us or our ministry. Every one of their calls is a great encouragement to us.

AVOID THE DANGERS

One of the celebrities I contacted regarding their personal intercessors sent me a letter rather than a list of personal prayer partners, expressing a degree of anxiety he had over the whole idea. I was surprised at this because it was such a new and exciting area for me. But soon afterward I spent some time with Pastor Casey Treat of the Christian Faith Center in Seattle, and he shared some background I had known nothing about.

In the early 1980s, a wave of fanaticism occurred concerning intercession, particularly among the "word of faith" charismatics, but also among other charismatics. Some pastors began to ride hobby horses and taught that if you did not pray three to five hours a day you were not moving in the Spirit. They picked up on Paul's "travail" or "laboring in birth" for the Galatians (see Gal. 4:19), and intercessors would groan loudly as if in labor and even lie on top of one another on the church platform. Another obvious example of flaky intercession. Some flaky fasting was also involved, based on the premise that the longer you fast the more you can get God to do what you want Him to do.

Fortunately, this was only a fad and is not seen much today. But Casey observes that the memories of this are still strong enough for some pastors to be very cautious about personal intercession. Casey Treat himself has a fine team of prayer partners. He introduced me personally to his three I-1 intercessors, each of whom has a particular specialization for their prayer ministry.

Even where the intercession itself is not flaky, dangers in receiving intercession need to be recognized and avoided. I have been stressing that personal intercession for pastors and other Christian leaders is a high-level spiritual activity. As such it attracts the attention of the devil in a high-level way. He will attack the relationship of a pastor and intercessors in any way possible, but he seems to focus on three principal areas: spiritual dependency, emotional dependency and physical dependency.

1. Spiritual Dependency

It is a big mistake for the pastor to become spiritually dependent on the intercessors. When this happens, the intercessor becomes a substitute for the pastor's own personal touch with the Lord. Judson Cornwall mentions this in his excellent book, *The Secret of Personal Prayer.* He says that as he traveled across America, "Often I found pastors dependent completely upon the prayers of a few old-timers, known as 'intercessors,' for the pastors themselves had virtually no private prayer ministry. This may well explain the staleness, the decline in morality, and the great insecurity that seems to characterize much of America's clergy."[10]

If you as a pastor feel you might be falling into the trap of cutting back on your personal prayer life, I suggest you do something about it. I spent a good bit of chapters 4 and 5 stressing the need for us as leaders to develop quality prayer lives of our own, precisely so we could avoid spiritual dependency. If it has been some time since you read them, I suggest you review those chapters.

Also read good books such as Judson Cornwall's *The Secret of Personal Prayer* (Creation House), Dick Eastman's *The Hour That Changes the World* (Baker), Wesley Duewel's *Mighty Prevailing Prayer* (Zondervan), B. J. Willhite's *Why Pray?* (Creation House), Donald Bloesch's *The Struggle of Prayer* (Harper & Row), Larry Lea's *Could You Not Tarry One Hour?* (Creation House) or Bill Hybels' *Too Busy Not to Pray* (InterVarsity).

It is one thing to wake up some morning and say, "Lord, I'm wiped out. Please let the intercessors carry the day." It is quite another to make a habit of doing this. No number or quality of intercessors can substitute for the pastor or other leader being an authentic man or woman of God.

2. Emotional Dependency

Cindy Jacobs warns, "The partners might become emotionally wrapped up in you, or you in them, in a way that is not healthy."[11] This does not mean you must not have a specially close relationship with one or more intercessors, but it does mean the relationship must at all times be an objective relationship.

If you find yourself down when the intercessor is down it can be a danger sign. The intercessor (unless it is the spouse or a close family member) should never become a focal point of personal happiness or fulfillment. To imagine, "If I lost my intercessor I wouldn't be able to go on in my ministry" is a sign of emotional dependency.

Some have used the term "emotional adultery." Physical adultery involves delivering your body to another; emotional adultery is delivering your soul. There is a line between friendship and affection. Crossing that line with an intercessor can lead to disaster.

3. Physical Dependency

I have said enough about immorality in the ministry to give us the impression it has become one of Satan's most effective tools in crippling the church in our day and age. It should come as no surprise to suggest that Satan would like to destroy relationships between pastors and intercessors through inappropriate physical contact.

Most cases of pastoral indiscretion have been sparked in the counseling relationship, contacts with staff members taking second place. I have not as yet heard of immoral physical relationships between pastors and intercessors, although I do know of one pastor's I-1 intercessor running off with the pastor's father.

Inappropriate contact is a constant danger that needs to be

understood and avoided. Research shows that the great majority of pastors are male and the great majority of intercessors are female. This situation is not likely to change in the near future.

To avoid the danger of wrong contacts totally, some pastors such as John Maxwell only relate to male prayer partners. It is not that either John or his wife, Margaret, have any kind of excessive phobia about John's relating to women in the general course of his pastoral ministry. He relates as well as any.

When I interviewed John about this danger he told me his policy is always to play to his strengths, and his strength is to lead men. His gifts are such that men enjoy following his leadership. Not only is he receiving intercession from the 100 men who are his intercessors, but he is also discipling them in their Christian faith. He calls his prayer partners his "farm team" for the church board. No one is nominated to the board who has not been a prayer partner.

Furthermore, John has rightly observed that in the average congregation women pray much more than men. In his congregation he wants as many men praying as women, so he directs his attention toward motivating and training men to pray. And it pays off. Remember the story in chapter 1 about hearing through the prayer partners, "This is not your site"?

John Maxwell does not teach that all pastors should have the same policy he has, but it goes without saying, many pastors should follow his example. Or they should recruit family members as intercessors.

MALE LEADERS AND FEMALE INTERCESSORS

For some, female intercessors for male leaders works well. I have mentioned that I believe two of Paul's intercessors were Euodia and Syntyche, both women. Having somewhat less evidence, I nevertheless suspect, as I have mentioned earlier, that

Mary, the mother of John Mark, could have been one of Peter's closest intercessors.

To cause physical dependency, the enemy uses lust, inappropriate language and inappropriate contact. In order to avoid any of this, common sense is needed. For one thing, the pastor must have a solid marriage as a prerequisite for relating to an I-1 intercessor of the opposite sex. There must be an open relationship between the spouses as well. The danger of physical indiscretion should be mutually recognized and assiduously avoided.

Cindy Jacobs says, "Do not meet with a member of the opposite sex for prayer without someone else being present."[12] I go so far as to say the less one-on-one contact there is between a leader and a member of the opposite sex in general the better. Having breakfast or lunch or driving from one place to another with a female intercessor is not recommended.

I was concerned, when I developed these rules for myself years ago, that I might be overly old-fashioned. But I was heartened by my friend Pastor Rick Warren of Saddleback Valley Community Church. He is a megachurch pastor in his 30s who has never been accused of being "old-fashioned." After the Jimmy Swaggart scandal broke, he laid down for his staff "Saddleback's Ten Commandments."

1. Thou shalt not visit the opposite sex alone at home.
2. Thou shalt not counsel the opposite sex alone at the office.
3. Thou shalt not counsel the opposite sex more than once without that person's mate.
4. Thou shalt not go to lunch alone with the opposite sex.
5. Thou shalt not kiss any attender of the opposite sex or show affection that could be questioned.

6. Thou shalt not discuss detailed sexual problems with the opposite sex in counseling.
7. Thou shalt not discuss your marriage problems with an attender of the opposite sex.
8. Thou shalt be careful in answering cards and letters from the opposite sex.
9. Thou shalt make your secretary your protective ally.
10. Thou shalt pray for the integrity of other staff members.

I have written out Rick Warren's rules in full because I think following them could avoid many of the problems we are having in the ministry today. I agree with them and I follow them myself. Not only do I want to avoid pitfalls such as physical dependency, I also want to avoid the appearance of evil.

Recognize the Role of the Intercessor
Both the leader and the intercessor should recognize that the role of the intercessor is:

- A close personal relationship, but not marriage
- A strong influence in the life of the leader, but not manipulation or control
- Partnership in ministry, but not ownership of ministry.

FWC "Pastor"

GO AND DO IT

Steven Johnson, president of World Indigenous Missions, took a missions course with me at Fuller. Several months later he wrote, reminding me that I had mentioned intercession and prayer partners rather briefly in class. I had encouraged those who did not have intercessors to go and do it.

He said, "As president of a world-wide church planting ministry I had found myself under severe spiritual attack. This resulted in extreme fatigue, the vexing of my soul, as well as spiritual attacks on my family." So Steve did it; he formed a team of prayer partners for the first time.

"Results of this were overwhelming," Johnson reports. "Within days of sending the letter, I sensed a tremendous lifting of spiritual oppressions. I sensed a freedom concerning a warfare that was attacking my family as well as my personal ministry." He attributes all of this to the power released by God through his prayer team.

"In these last ten months," he says, "I can give testimony to being significantly different than the months and years prior to having this prayer team."

Why not be like Steve Johnson? Go and do it!

■ REFLECTION QUESTIONS ■

1. What can we learn from the apostle Paul's attitudes toward his personal intercessors?
2. Why is it that the leader needs to pray for the intercessors but not as much as the intercessors pray for the leader?
3. Discuss the three danger areas of spiritual, emotional and physical dependency.
4. Do you think Rick Warren's "Saddleback's Ten Commandments" are too strict? Why?
5. Discuss plans you personally have to implement some of the things you have learned from this book.

Just simply the entire body function together with all its parts including Intercession.

Notes

1. Clinton E. Arnold, *Ephesians: Power and Magic* (Cambridge, England: Cambridge University Press, 1989), p. 1.
2. Rolf Zettersten, *Dr. Dobson: Turning Hearts Toward Home* (Dallas, TX: WORD INC., 1989), p. 65.
3. Ibid., p. 169.
4. Reinhard Bonnke, *Evangelism by Fire* (Eastbourne, England: Kingsway Publications, 1989), p. 217.
5. This information was gleaned from a personal letter from Suzette Hattingh (March 23, 1992).
6. Eileen Crossman, *Mountain Rain* (Robesonia, PA: OMF Books, 1982), p. 65.
7. Ibid., p. 64.
8. J. O. Fraser, *The Prayer of Faith* (Robesonia, PA: OMF Books, 1958), p. 12.
9. Cindy Jacobs, *Possessing the Gates of the Enemy* (Tarrytown, NY: Chosen Books, 1991), p. 165.
10. Judson Cornwall, *The Secret of Personal Prayer* (Altamonte Springs, FL: Creation House, 1988), pp. 9-10.
11. Jacobs, *Possessing the Gates*, p. 165.
12. Ibid., p. 166.

PRAYER

INDEX

SHIELD

 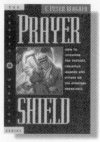 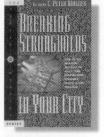 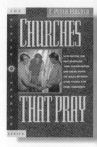
  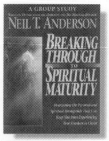